# HOMES & COURTYARDS

28 Beautifully Designed Homes For Outdoor Living

# HOMES & COURTYARDS

## 28 Beautifully Designed Homes For Outdoor Living

BASSENIAN / LAGONI ARCHITECTS

Library of Congress Control Number:
2007924321

International Standard Book Number:
978-0-9721539-3-5 (hardcover)
0-9721539-3-4 (hardcover)

Published by Bassenian/Lagoni Architects
2031 Orchard Drive, Suite 100
Newport Beach, CA 92660-0753
Phone: 949-553-9100
Fax: 949-553-0548
www.bassenianlagoni.com

Corporate
Chairman & CEO: Aram Bassenian, AIA
President: Carl Lagoni, AIA
Executive Vice President: Jeffrey LaFetra, AIA
Chief Financial Officer: Lee Rogaliner
Senior Principals: Scott Adams, AICP
                David Kosco, AIA
                Jeff Lake, AIA
Principals: Ali Badie, AIA
                Steven Dewan, AIA
                Kevin Karami
                Ken Niemerski, AIA

Book Production
Editorial Director: Aram Bassenian, AIA
Editor-in-Chief: Rickard Bailey, Bailey Consulting, Inc.
Editor: Heather McCune
Writer: Laura Hurst Brown, Rascal Words, Ltd.
Design/Art Director: Edie Motoyama
Art Director/Designer, Cover Design: Zareh Marzbetuny, ZM Design
Floor Plan Graphics: Stacie Arrigo, Jennifer Cram, Edie Motoyama
Assistants to the Editorial Director: Kele Dooley, Debby Owens

Prepress by Toppan Hong Kong

Printed in China by Toppan Printing

10  9  8  7  6  5  4  3  2  1

# Contents

# Acknowledgements

BY ARAM BASSENIAN, AIA

Publishing has taken us on a rapid and eventful journey. It has been only two years since the publication of our second book, *Tuscan and Andalusian Reflections*, and just four years since we published our first volume, *Pure California*. Now, in *Homes and Courtyards*, we present our most extensive architectural work to date, with many of the homes emphasizing outdoor living. Such design evolution is our response to the changing needs of a robust economy in the United States and in emerging economies worldwide. There seems to be a clear recognition that home ownership is a substantial economic pillar in any growing society. To this we attribute a part of our success and for this we are thankful.

At Bassenian/Lagoni Architects, we cultivate a problem-solving and practical design attitude. Our company culture dictates that constraints are mere opportunities to be exploited for new and dynamic architecture. We firmly believe that our role is to assist the development team; thus, to us, excellence in service is a daily mantra. Therefore, we express our deep appreciation to a very unique team of talented professionals who constitute our firm. It is only the very passionate and mature design professional who has the ability to step up, time and time again, to offer fresh and diverse solutions—and we salute those in our office who do just that on a daily basis.

We are indebted as well to many of our clients, both builder and marketing executives, whose vision begins the design process for these beautiful homes and communities. They are courageous "place-makers" in the full sense of the definition. And our gratitude extends to their project managers and construction teams who embrace this vision and, through commitment and hard work, complete the mission with excellence.

We also extend sincere appreciation to our allied professionals—the structural engineers, landscape architects and interior designers who help make every new home an unfolding chapter in the American dream. It is only through total commitment to their craft that sticks and stones turn to comfort and elegance.

Lastly and importantly, I am forever indebted to my enlightened parents who willingly, and at a late age, sacrificed all to bring their children to this "shining city on the hill." Along the way they demonstrated the virtues of work, yet taught me moderation and balance in all matters of life. I am so grateful to America for affording me and my family education and, therefore, endless opportunity. And, closest to home, my deepest appreciation goes to my family for giving my life true purpose, guidance and stability.

# Foreword

*This is what I prayed for … a piece of land — not so very big,
with a garden and, near the house, a spring that never fails,
and a bit of wood to round it off.*

— Horace

Now, more than 20 centuries later, we live at a pace Horace could not have imagined in 30 B.C. In our 24/7 world, with more gadgets, Google Earth, ways to design a car or plan a vacation on-line, we multi-task to manage work, family, pets, aging parents, what to eat for dinner, and, of course, e-mail. But much like Horace, we dream about a home, *our* home on our land, a place of beauty, respite, warmth, at one with nature, a place that's right for us.

Bassenian/Lagoni Architects' magic is in creating right places. Their homes give us refuge from the hectic world and shelter in its deepest, best meaning. They ground us in the land, the courtyard gardens, the beautiful interior spaces and the diverse exteriors that enrich the neighborhoods where they are built.

Frederic March, in his book, *Thunder at Twilight*, noted that all great places have two things in common: one foot in memory and one foot in prophecy. Bassenian/Lagoni imbues their architecture with that truth — creating homes that embody the best traditions of design — through materials, proportions and architectural styles. At the same time, their work embraces and celebrates the future with clean lines, simple elegance and artful form, bringing the art in architecture to every home.

In traveling the globe, from Tuscan Italy to Moorish Spain, and from the New England coast to the American Southwest, Bassenian/Lagoni designers have tapped into the world-influences on great architecture. And they've drawn on the best of America's rich residential heritage. From Neff to Maybeck and from Gill to Wright, their work weaves together memory and prophecy.

The noted mid-century California architect, Cliff May, once designed a two-room house with a five-room garden. The courtyard homes displayed in this volume honor the notion of that connectivity. Natural light seems to penetrate each of these homes so seamlessly. Whether it is an expansive veranda or a central courtyard, the outdoors consistently activates the core and elements of each of these houses with inventiveness. Outdoor living truly has an allure all of its own and these wondrous homes blend the dreams of the owner and architect with the land and garden. Bassenian/Lagoni's work accentuates that combination in its creative best—*right places*.

As a child, I grew up on Prospect Boulevard in Pasadena — one of the streets mentioned in Allan Jacobs' *Great Streets* classic. From the camphor-tree canopy to the Wallace Neff, Greene and Greene, and Frank Lloyd Wright homes, my neighborhood was filled with architectural gems and landscape grandeur. As a youngster, I took it for granted that all neighborhoods were this wonderful. It spoiled me for the future – and made other right places so much more valuable when I found them.

In the pages of this book, you'll see homes that are distinctive and that resonate with the feeling of *right place* for the right homeowner. Therein lies the practical genius of Bassenian/Lagoni Architects' work. Whether designing a one-family custom home, like the Wine Country Residence in Paso Robles, or a whole development neighborhood, like Bella Fioré in Lake Las Vegas, Bassenian/Lagoni Architects create homes as different and distinctive as their owners, things of beauty with extraordinary character and appeal…*right places*. And like the great neighborhoods of the past, I long to live in one. That's their magic.

# Introduction

TRADITION AND INNOVATION

BY ARAM BASSENIAN, AIA & CARL LAGONI, AIA

INTRODUCTION :: 11

Tradition and innovation – two seemingly contradictory influences – often contribute equally to the architecture that shapes our lives. Consider the following definitions:

**Tradition:** an inherited, established customary pattern of thought, action or behavior; the handing down of information, beliefs, and customs from one generation to another without written instruction.

**Innovation:** the introduction of something new; to effect a change in something.

Architecture consistently draws inspiration from the past and modifies the original to express a new aesthetic that reflects current ways of thinking. Historical influences for our work have come from masters such as:

*Andrea Palladio*, one of the most influential architects in the Western world, was prolific in Northern Italy during the sixteenth century. Drawing great inspiration from classical architecture, he generated a carefully proportioned vocabulary that became the model for stately homes and government buildings in both Europe and in America.

*Wallace Neff* was instrumental in his impact on Southern California's early residential architecture. Reflecting the Moorish idioms of the Mediterranean climate zone, his homes designed for movie moguls appeared in the 1930s. Today, they are the epitome of that era with an eloquence untainted by the passage of time.

To architect *Charles Moore* we credit the ignition of the more playful Post-Modern movement. The significance of his contribution is immeasurable. Through him, in part, modernism was rapidly transformed, allowing architects freedom for open experimentation.

*Ricardo Legorreta*, a noted designer from Mexico, has authored an architectural language that combines bold, clean, colorful forms with the character of the Southwest. His work stands out for its simplicity and sculptural singularity.

These masters create designs so substantive that they seem to transcend time and place. As architects who follow, our role is to understand the essence of their work and, using today's technology and building materials, create up-to-date homes reflective of contemporary lifestyle.

Today, as a firm, we find ourselves practicing during a unique time in history. Buoyed by an expanding economy, we have multiple opportunities for creativity. At the same time, our design efforts are occurring in a highly competitive marketplace. This milieu fuels advancement and evolution — motivating us to continuously reach for the next and more sophisticated home. And through our involvement with development housing, we are gratified to touch so many in America as they pursue their home-ownership dream.

In the following pages we unveil homes that represent our current contribution to the evolving art form that is housing. With ordered architecture, fractured massing and brick and stone detailing, we recall the hill towns of Tuscany at *Castellina*. The interiors of these upscale townhomes are designed to naturally flow out to balconies, loggias and extended patios to enthusiastically connect with the soft climate of coastal Southern California.

At the *Shady Canyon Residence*, a layering of spaces is unveiled through controlled openings. A progression unfolds to reveal the spatial experiences of this unique home. Formal and informal as well as indoor and outdoor living areas are contained with unity in a rural Mediterranean theme.

The *Wine Country Residence* in Paso Robles rests on a spectacular hilltop. Combine this great site with the ideal client and you have the once-in-a-lifetime opportunity for any architectural firm. Here with crisp, contemporary lines and inspiration from Legorreta, the front and back of this dwelling open to meet the vineyards of central California.

And it all comes together at *The Tides* in Newport Coast. Residential architecture, with inspiration from Tuscany, turns to express a new aesthetic in upscale coastal living. An entry forecourt, followed by a three-story interior courtyard, is enhanced by exquisite brick and stone detailing, bringing the outdoors inside and stimulating our senses.

As you experience this photographic home tour with its attendant narrative, we hope you find in our homes and communities a respect for tradition with a flare that speaks of innovation.

CHAPTER ONE

HOMES & COURTYARDS

# The Tides

BUILDER: STANDARD PACIFIC HOMES • LOCATION: NEWPORT COAST, CALIFORNIA • PHOTOGRAPHY: ANTHONY GOMEZ

RESIDENCE ONE

Perched above a breathtaking stretch of the Pacific coastline, this richly detailed Mediterranean home captures the strong lines of a classic Tuscan farmhouse. Just beyond the formal entry forecourt, the house reveals its dramatic surprise: a stunning three-story second courtyard that allows sunlight and coastal breezes to penetrate and infuse the center of this magnificent home. As the sequence of spaces unfolds, the building takes shape with well-delineated mixes of stone and stucco that visually connect the house with the coastal grandeur of the site. Vistas extend beyond the rear loggia and terrace to the horizon, where glimpses of the sea confer a sense of tranquility on the home. Public rooms on the main and lower levels relate closely to the subterranean garden, a refreshing counterpoint to the rustic sophistication of the interior. Open to the sky, the courtyards complement exposure to the outdoors at the front and rear of the home, and lend light and protection from the elements at its core.

**Right** | Worthy of its upscale location, the house achieves visual continuity with the site and opens to an uninterrupted vista that extends from the sidewalk to the sea. Despite its apparent size and grandeur, the home contains an elegant floor plan that lives principally on one level.

**Below** | Centuries collide at the rear perimeter, where detailed brick surrounds, stone cladding and a trio of arches play against the clean lines of a very up-to-date home. A ribbon of vertical windows flanking the upper loggia captures vast views of the sea.

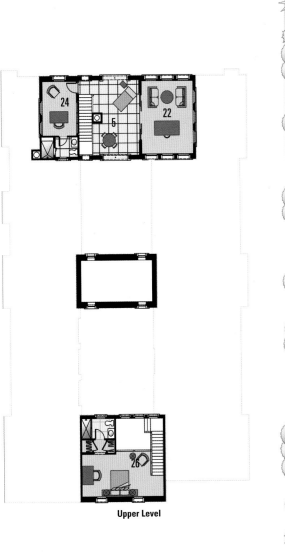

**Upper Level**

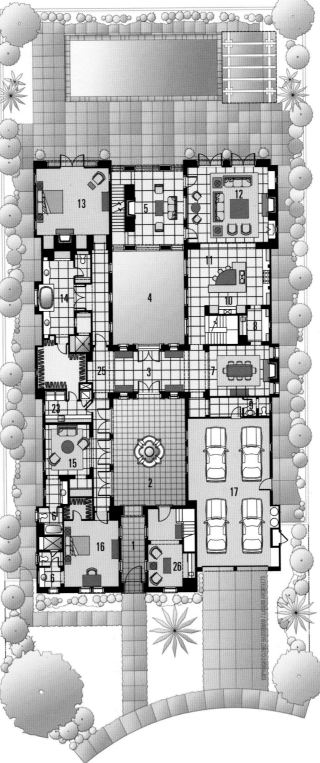

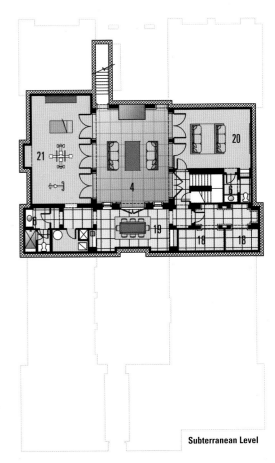

**Subterranean Level**

**About The Floor Plan:** Influenced by rural Mediterranean antecedents, the plan is defined by groups of simple, rectilinear shapes. Oriented toward the sea, the house opens at the entry foyer to a finely crafted central courtyard, offering an unexpected view of the whole house. With livability focused on the main floor, the home is enhanced with a two-story casita at the entry, an artist loft and office on the upper floor, and a fitness room, wine cellar and home theater below.

## Legend

| | | |
|---|---|---|
| 1 Breezeway | 10 Kitchen | 19 Wine Tasting Room |
| 2 Forecourt | 11 Nook | 20 Home Theater |
| 3 Foyer | 12 Family Room | 21 Fitness Room |
| 4 Central Courtyard | 13 Master Bedroom | 22 Artist Loft |
| 5 Loggia | 14 Master Bathroom | 23 Laundry |
| 6 Bathroom | 15 Den | 24 Office |
| 7 Dining Room | 16 Bedroom Suite | 25 Gallery Hall |
| 8 Butler's Pantry | 17 Garage | 26 Casita |
| 9 Powder Room | 18 Wine Cellar | |

**7,171 SQUARE FEET**

**Opposite Page** | Hand-applied plaster finishes, exposed rafter tails and flourishes of wrought iron reference elements of rural Italian villas at the courtyard. An open foyer overlooks the central courtyard, which functions as an outdoor living area, linked to a wine cellar and wine tasting room via French doors.

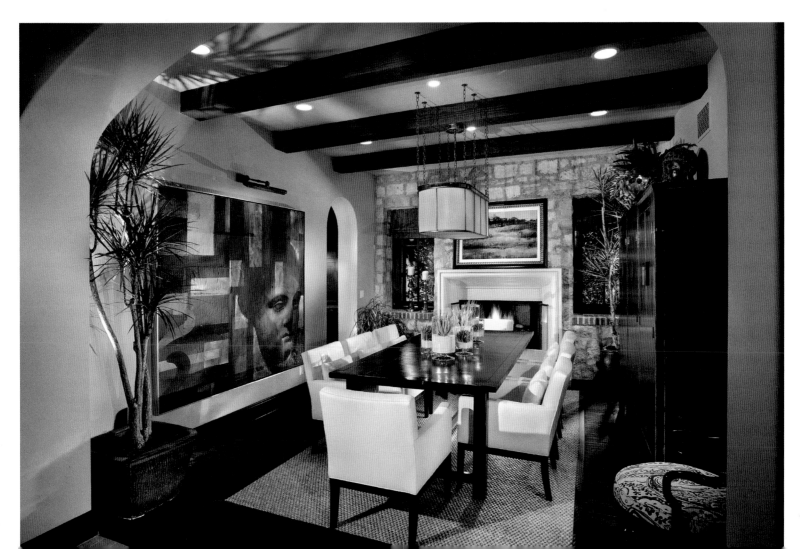

**Opposite Page Above** | An intimately scaled foyer intersects the plan at the entry, creating a spatial connection between the forecourt and the central courtyard, and linking the formal and private wings of the home.

**Opposite Page Below** | A fusion of coastal influences creates a striking balance of clean, cosmopolitan lines and rural character in the formal dining room. The muted palette of sand-pebble hues provides an ideal canvas for the space's more striking furnishings.

**Above** | Rough stone walls and a timber ceiling alter the depth and dimension of the informal living area viewed from the open kitchen. A scalloped, square arch adds subtle definition to the space, accentuated by a shift to hardwood from travertine floors.

**Above** | Open to views of the ocean, the master bedroom offers a seamless boundary to the rear terrace, pool and deck. The deep, umber tones of the hardwood floor are contradicted by the sleek lines of a marble fireplace surround.

**Below Left** | The vintage garden tub sets the tone in the master bath, which offers splendid amenities, such as a walk-through closet, separate lavs and vanities, and a step-in dual shower.

**Above** | Sliding French doors open the upper-level artist's loft to the upper loggia, where wide views of the horizon are absorbed by the interior. Three windows—like ship's portals—bring in natural light and long thoughts of the sea.

**Below Right** | Timber trusses and a flagstone deck add dimension and color to a partially enclosed sitting area at the upper loggia. Ocean breezes flow through the space even when the drapes are closed.

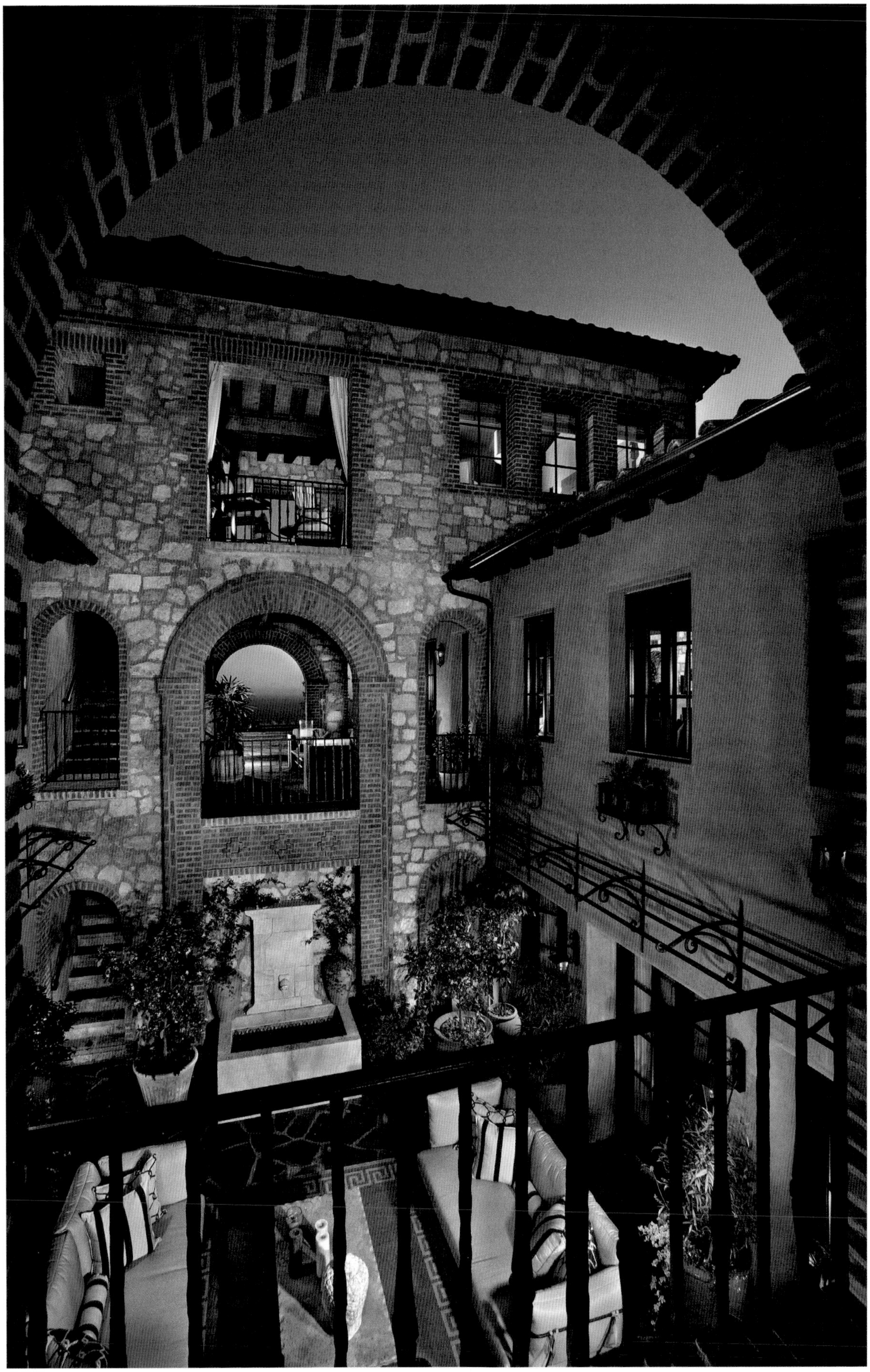

**Opposite Page** | The purity of the design stems from the symmetry that is evident at the central courtyard—a playful, unexpected element that brings light into the core of the home. Varied textures of wood, stone, timber and brick soften the scale of the home, and call up ageless traditions that add depth to its character.

**Right** | French doors open the house to the amenities of the back property, a fitting environment for owners who love the outdoors. A blend of natural materials—clay roof tiles and timber beams—authenticate the elevation's rural theme.

**Above** | Located near the top of a hillside, the waters of a lap pool appear to rise to the level of the sea. An extensive terrace provides unobstructed views for lounging sunbathers.

**Below** | At the edge of the rear property, a pergola shelters an outdoor eating area, adjacent to an alfresco kitchen packed with luxe amenities such as dual commercial-grade grills.

**Above** | At the rear elevation, a simple stone-clad central mass is flanked by single-story stucco structures, evoking the scale of early Tuscan homes. A covered staircase connects the levels of a two-story loggia that increases light and circulation throughout the plan.

# Bella Fioré
## at Lake Las Vegas

BUILDER: PARDEE HOMES • LOCATION: HENDERSON, NEVADA
PHOTOGRAPHY: ERIC FIGGE

## THE COMMUNITY

Set against the wide-open scenery of the high desert, this community of courtyard homes overlooks the jagged outcroppings of hillsides surrounding an area well within view of the famed Las Vegas Strip. Influenced by Andalusian, Tuscan and Italian Renaissance design themes, the houses employ cultured stone and barrel tile to create harmonious links to the environment. A stone's throw from the amenities of Lake Las Vegas Resort, the neighborhood is a natural extension of the waterfront community, with a precisely orchestrated look that pairs recessed entries, forecourts and courtyards with the varied rooflines of a village environment. One- and two-story elevations engage well-scaled proportions and traditional details—bracketed cornices, classic brick arches, overhanging eaves and sculpted columns—to underscore their link to the past, yet the homes are flexible, highly functional and environmentally friendly. Walls of glass convey a pleasing sense of space inside, integrating wide panels of scenery with rooms that also provide a sense of protection and shelter.

**Above** | Elemental materials, varied rooflines and broken massing create a gracious, human-scaled elevation, invigorated by textured planes, deeply recessed windows and a bold tower that harbors the entry.

**Opposite Page Above** | Granite-slab countertops and maple cabinetry complement sleek stainless-steel appliances in a gourmet kitchen designed for two cooks. A sculpted passageway leads to the formal dining room through a well-equipped butler's pantry.

**Opposite Page Center** | An open arrangement of the family room, morning nook and kitchen creates interplay between the cool polished tones of the food-preparation area and the cultivated look of the rear garden.

**Opposite Page Below** | Views extend beyond the rear perimeter to a spacious yard that repeats the pure, linear dimensions of the house. A covered loggia unites the master wing with an informal eating area, exemplifying the home's indoor-outdoor aesthetic.

**Opposite Page Above** | Amenities in the spa-like master bath include a step-in dual shower, a garden tub and a well-organized walk-in closet. A leaded-glass window and a recessed vanity affirm the lush character of the owners' retreat.

**Opposite Page Center** | In the gourmet kitchen, paneled cabinetry and a midnight-black tiled backsplash contribute to the European feel of the home. A crescent-shaped island orients the work spaces toward the morning room and overlooks the back property.

**Above** | Pure-white brackets and overhanging eaves play counterpoint to a barrel-tile roof and Venetian-red plaster on an elaborate façade derived from the villas of Italy. The forecourt leads to a foyer and an inviting transition to the formal living spaces.

**Opposite Page Below** | Stepped massing at the rear elevation creates separation of the outside spaces, which include a quiet courtyard accessed from the living room. Transom windows accentuate the curved wall of glass that brightens the vaulted family room.

# Shady Canyon Residence

LOCATION: IRVINE, CALIFORNIA • PHOTOGRAPHY: ERIC FIGGE

Within a master-planned community fringed by a nature preserve and surrounded by coastal wilderness, the rubble-stone elevation of this custom courtyard home captures the spirit of a rugged Tuscan farmhouse. At the front of the plan, a 1½-story presentation conveys the simplicity of a rural villa and assigns a human scale to the streetscene. An understated forecourt allows glimpses of the central courtyard from the outside, and adds depth and dimension to a processional approach to the formal entry. Anchored by a central turret, the two-story rear elevation frames the central courtyard, which activates the primary living areas, infusing the rooms with natural light. Defined by a series of open spaces, the courtyard is enhanced with pavers and small gardens, and fused by a palette of natural materials. Inside, half-walls and flagstone steps combine with stairs and arches to define the multiple levels. At the upper courtyard, the steel-and-glass doors of a home office open on a graveled path that crosses to a covered court. Four steps lead to a lower-level fountain court that visually extends the casual living areas. Rooms on the upper floor benefit from the union of light and air brought in by a Juliet balcony overlooking the outdoor arena.

**About The Floor Plan:** A rectangular footprint encircles a courtyard that penetrates the plan on two levels, unified by a textured elevation of brick, stone and stucco. Single-level wings to the front of the plan provide both public and private spaces: a home office, guest quarters and a game room. To the rear of the plan, first-floor rooms radiate from a rotunda and stairwell, and lead to an open arrangement in the informal zone.

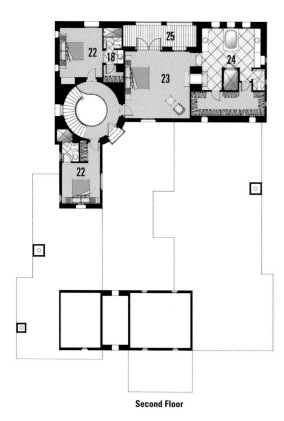

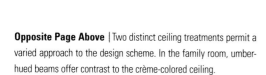

**Second Floor**

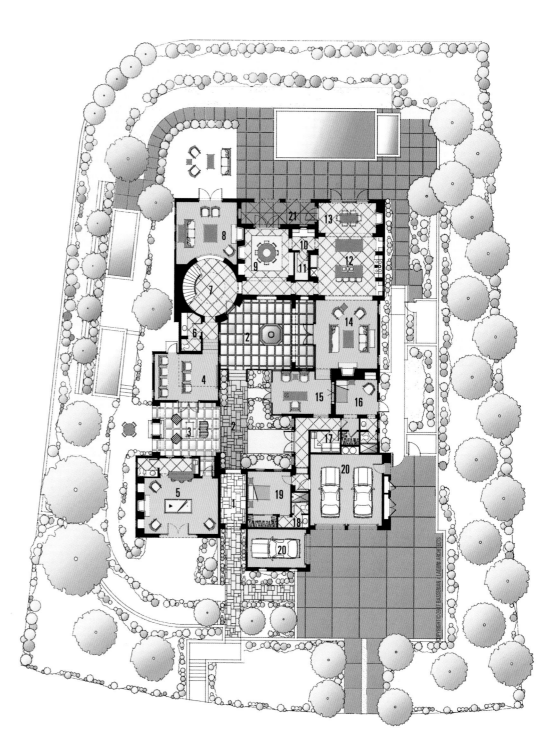

**Opposite Page Above** | Two distinct ceiling treatments permit a varied approach to the design scheme. In the family room, umber-hued beams offer contrast to the crème-colored ceiling.

**Opposite Page Below** | The linear proportions of the kitchen and morning nook are offset by rugged timbers and a plank ceiling above a wall of golden fieldstone. An arch of stacked brick articulates the boundary between the serving and eating areas.

**Previous Page** | Brick, stone, wood and iron dominate the public view of the central courtyard. Sequestered by a massive entry door, a narrow forecourt is framed by two rugged fieldstone piers and a brick arch.

## Legend

| | | | |
|---|---|---|---|
| 1 Forecourt | 8 Living Room | 15 Home Office | 22 Bedroom |
| 2 Central Courtyard | 9 Dining Room | 16 Maid's Room | 23 Master Bedroom |
| 3 Covered Courtyard | 10 Butler's Pantry | 17 Laundry | 24 Master Bathroom |
| 4 Home Theater | 11 Walk-in Pantry | 18 Bathroom | 25 Deck/Balcony |
| 5 Game Room | 12 Kitchen | 19 Guest Bedroom | |
| 6 Powder Room | 13 Morning Room | 20 Garage | |
| 7 Entry Rotunda | 14 Family Room | 21 Loggia | |

5,791 SQUARE FEET

**Above** | Playful lines at the entry artfully define the separation of the upper and lower floors. Corridor views extend the transitions to the living room and a gallery hall.

**Right** | The change in levels from the entry rotunda to the living room creates a purposeful division of space at the center of the home. An intimate grouping encircles the fireplace, which offsets the subdued spirit of the room with a commanding stone surround.

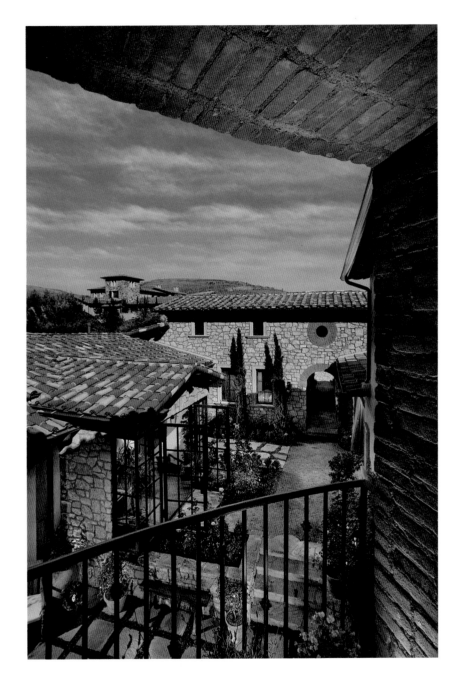

**Above** | Terracotta tile rooftops set among groves of cypress and olive trees bring to mind clusters of rural Italian houses perched on a scenic crest above the sea. The house is set in a community encompassing acres of canyons, hills and open spaces.

**Opposite Page** | A merger of house and garden occurs in the courtyard, where tile and stone create a unifying simplicity. French doors open the secluded home office to contemplative surroundings. Four steps down, an elegant stone fountain aligns with a set of glass doors leading to the family room.

**Above** | A covered side courtyard with an alfresco fireplace harbors an informal conversation group, adjacent to the home theater and a few steps from the game room. Heavy timber beams line the ceiling of this open-air room, designed to be simpatico with fieldstone walls and a floor of weathered-brick pavers.

**Below** | An olive tree casts shadows on the quiet side terrace and herb garden, where architectural forms of stone and tile step into the landscape. The through-fireplace is shared by the courtyard adjacent to the media room.

**Above** | Oriented toward the rear property, the upper-level master suite opens to a private deck with wide views of the preserved open spaces. Rough-hewn plank and beam ceilings contribute to the provincial charm of the owners' retreat, which provides a through-fireplace to the dual bath.

**Below** | Deep windows and recessed arches punctuate the two-story rear elevation. The simple rectangular massing is reminiscent of rural Mediterranean farmhouses. A covered loggia shelters an outdoor sitting area from the glare of the noonday sun.

# Elements of Design

## Exterior Materials To The Inside

■ Eminently livable inside and out, this fresh interpretation of a rustic field-stone villa imparts a sense of the past to a comfortable home infused with a modern aesthetic. Tuned to the natural setting, the Tuscan-style plan introduces structural and design elements that create pleasing adjacencies with traditional materials. Rough-hewn corbels set off craggy stone piers and brick-laden arches in the courtyard, a theme that is repeated indoors with heavy timbers, ledgestone, tile and bricks. A steady play of natural materials throughout the interior erases the distinction between even the formal rooms and the outdoors. A purposeful confrontation of elements occurs at boundary transitions from the courtyard to refined areas of the home: the entry rotunda, for example, exhibits a vibrant mix of renaissance themes, with thick Roman arches, terracotta pavers, sculpted wrought-iron balusters and mosaic stair tiles. Sleek metal-and-glass doors affirm the contemporary nature of the home office and media room. Every corner of the home exhibits warmth and vitality made tangible by the presence of natural exterior materials. The primal qualities of each room reconcile a needed sense of safety and shelter with the innate pleasures of living outdoors.

# Tremezzo at Lake Las Vegas

BUILDER: PARDEE HOMES • LOCATION: HENDERSON, NEVADA • PHOTOGRAPHY: ERIC FIGGE

## RESIDENCE TWO

Overlooking Lake Las Vegas, this Mediterranean retreat encircles a central courtyard, open to the sky and wrapped by a tile-roofed colonnade. At the front of the home, a strong, weathered-brick turret harbors a vaulted portico that creates passage to the formal entrance through the forecourt. Asymmetrical rooflines establish a varied rhythm for the façade, so that the house appears to be formed by many buildings, simulating a hilltown structure. An L-shaped loggia, defined by spiral columns and wide, sculpted arches, lines the private core of the home and articulates the positive outside space. A gallery and open rooms are organized around the center court, amplifying circulation and increasing light throughout the plan. A spacious great room extends the ambience of the courtyard to the covered patio via double sets of French doors. Surrounded by fairways and within walking distance of Lake Las Vegas village, the master-down home offers a resort environment with plenty of room for friends and visitors. Interior living spaces offer site lines oriented toward wide views captured through walls of glass. The informality of the home is expressed by the order and versatility of the interior spaces: a family room or media center off the patio, a morning room adjoining the courtyard, a flexible, upper-level club room and a main-level home office that converts to a theater, den or fourth bedroom.

## Legend

| | | |
|---|---|---|
| 1 Entry Portal | 7 Morning Room | 13 Master Bedroom |
| 2 Loggia | 8 Laundry | 14 Master Bathroom |
| 3 Central Courtyard | 9 Family Room | 15 Bedroom |
| 4 Living Room | 10 Garage | 16 Guest Suite |
| 5 Dining Room | 11 Gallery Hall | 17 Home Theater |
| 6 Kitchen | 12 Powder Room | 18 Club Room |

3,726 SQUARE FEET

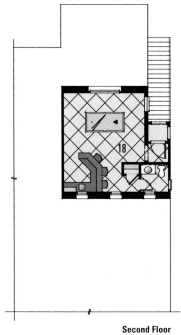

**Second Floor**

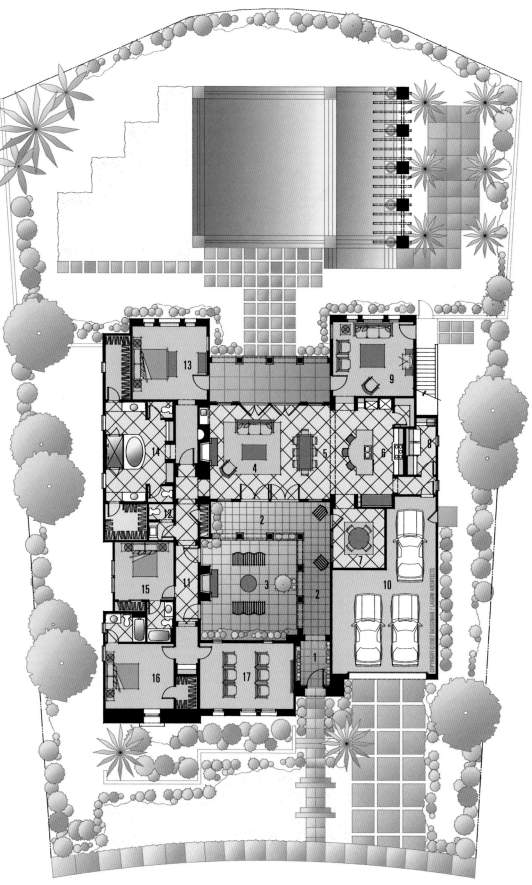

**About The Floor Plan:** Designed as a second home for grown families and empty-nesters, the 1½-story plan combines an informal arrangement of rooms with a large, central courtyard. Seamless transitions to the outside are provided by rows of French doors, which integrate the rear patio into the home. Near the master retreat, secondary suites are granted access to the courtyard via a gallery hall. An exterior staircase leads up to a club room that offers a grand view of the pool and spa and converts to guest quarters.

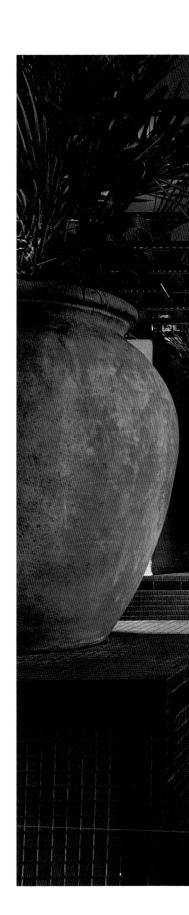

**Above** | Spiral columns and massive arches frame the center courtyard, anchored by an outdoor fireplace and wrapped with a loggia that shelters and subdues the space between the open-air living area and the house.

**Right** | Fractured massing at the rear elevation reveals Mediterranean instincts with a colonnade and a ribbon of clerestory windows. A shallow underwater deck permits the pool to lap the feet of a line of chaise lounges.

# Casa Bonita del Rio

LOCATION: RANCHO SANTA FE, CALIFORNIA • PHOTOGRAPHY: ERIC FIGGE

Historic Rancho Santa Fe provides a perfect backdrop to the Early California theme of this one-of-a-kind home. Like an early-day *casa de pueblo*, a subdued entry framed by a vintage, Mission-style façade conceals a highly livable retreat of high-beamed ceilings, rustic stone arches and cool tiled floors. Mission influences inspired by the original masterworks of such regional luminaries as Wallace Neff and Lilian Rice translate easily to the open-air galleries of this single-level plan. Set on ten acres, the home fully engages its surroundings with outdoor entertainment areas, including a lush pool-and-spa environment and two loggias that ease the transitions from indoors to out. Sight lines extend the width of the house in two directions from the entry rotunda along the spine of the home, and offer engaging vistas of the back property. Flourishes of desert hues and rugged textures assign an authentic character to the home—a hacienda-style ranch house with strong ties to the outdoors. Vaulted arches add a wealth of character to individual rooms without detracting from the visual harmony and fluent dimensions that unite the home with its natural setting. Rows of windows bring in broad panels of scenery throughout the home, while along the rear perimeter, sliding glass walls achieve a seamless integration with the landscape.

**Above** | Heavy timber beams play harmony with a series of clerestory windows designed to offer privacy and glimpses of daylight. A brick archway frames a tranquil view of the front courtyard and fountain.

**Previous Page** | Varied rooflines accentuate the massing of the elevation, an asymmetrical arrangement of forms anchored by a central entry turret. A carved door opens to the *portal*, or entry hall, derived from Mission dialects.

**Opposite Page** | High-volume planked ceilings expand the vertical dimensions of the informal zone, a flexible entertainment area linked to the back property via a wide loggia. A raised-hearth fireplace with an intricately decorated tile surround offers a visual foil to the grand scale of the space.

# Rimrock Summit

BUILDER: MASTERCRAFT HOMES
LOCATION: HIDDEN MEADOWS, CALIFORNIA • PHOTOGRAPHY: LANCE GORDON

## THE COMMUNITY

This resort-style hilltop neighborhood caters to upscale professionals, employing a diverse architectural scheme, tailored amenities, flexible interiors and views that stretch westward to Catalina Island. Set in hilly terrain pocketed with boulders and swaths of chaparral, houses orient toward the distant sea, with outdoor retreats that overlook olive groves and other indigenous growth. Santa Barbara and Tuscan exterior styles with a menu of floor plans and options alter the look and function of individual homes, and create a custom-home feel throughout the community. The plans feature formal entries, stair halls and large public rooms, many of which capture the fifty-mile vista. Arched windows, precast-stone columns, brick turrets and hipped roofs contribute to design authenticity. Forecourts, porticos, casitas and sheltered porches reinforce the architectural expressions. Inside, open arrangements of the living and dining rooms, with vaulted foyers and balcony overlooks, complement impressive informal areas that connect easily with the outdoors. Versatile spaces—game rooms, dens, home offices and guest quarters—are marked by open archways and easy transitions that promote the function and flow of the homes.

**Below** | The open arrangement of the family room and kitchen, with a subtle sense of separation provided by a square arch, creates striking interior vistas. Paneled walls reference the kitchen's cherry-colored wood cabinetry and hardwood floors, visually uniting the area.

**Opposite Page Top** | A trio of clerestory glass panes allows glimpses of sky above a Palladian-style window that enriches the living room with views of the horizon. A sculpted arch opens the space to the formal dining room; the through-fireplace is shared with the adjacent den.

**Opposite Page Center** | The upper-level master suite provides a sitting area that opens to an expansive deck through a single French door. Light and views permitted by the large panel of windows enhance the connection to the outdoors.

**Opposite Page Bottom** | A series of arches creates a site line from the entry to the family room. Designed as a casual gathering space and command-central for traditional events, the kitchen offers flexible dining options.

# Castellina at Covenant Hills

BUILDER: CENTEX HOMES • LOCATION: LADERA RANCH, CALIFORNIA • PHOTOGRAPHY: ERIC FIGGE

## TOWNHOMES & FLATS

Stacked stone, terracotta tile and ochre-colored stucco call up the rugged, earthen forms of Italy's hill country in this prominent neighborhood of flats and townhomes. Streets follow the quiet contours of slopes and banks that wind through the community and conclude in idyllic destinations: circular piazzas wrapped by cul-de-sacs that layer even the primary traffic arteries with a sense of nature. Village trails link to parks and public spaces and maintain a friendly dialogue with the landscape. Tuscan-inspired exteriors reflect a spirited style yet express an affinity for the rural themes of the Italian originals. Multifaceted forms typify the low-pitched lines and fractured massing of the Mediterranean design, redefined as a diverse network of attached villas. Hipped and gabled rooftops and asymmetrical forms create a rhythm that tempers the scale of the structures and preserves a sense of intimacy. The imposing geometry is punctuated by rows of windows that open the homes to light and views. Covered loggias, verandas and decks invite the natural environment into the public and informal zones, and function well as outdoor rooms.

**Below** | Interlocking buildings carve out privacy and individuality, while integrating the interiors with natural light and views. Clusters of townhomes feature varied entry and garage configurations to reinforce a strategy of privacy.

**Previous Page** | A playful informality prevails at the rear perimeter, where a series of courtyard-like settings enliven the balance of stucco, brick and wood. Fractured massing produces natural clusters of townhomes and flats, creating patterned angles of light that activate the individual units.

**Opposite Page** | Recessed double-sash windows set off a balance of stucco and stone on the exterior elevations, which swing side-loading garages away from the street thus reducing the dominance of the garage doors.

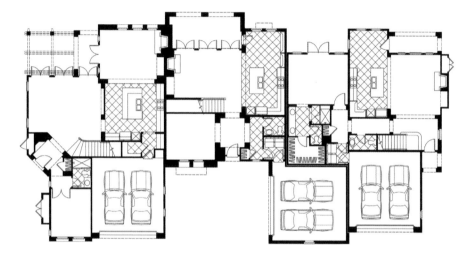

**About The Floor Plan:** Situated on an elevated site, the community contains 82 homes on approximately 11 acres, an arrangement that takes advantage of wonderful views. Organized into scaled neighborhoods by a spine street and its tributaries, the community also uses portal-type entry roads and sloped banks encircling land masses to further define its softscape boundaries. Two different building types offer varied elevations: two-story luxury plexes with individual covered loggias and verandas; and flats and multi-story units—such as a tri-level design with a loft retreat—linked to decks and verandas.

**Above Left** | The central element of this single-story floor plan is the formal dining room, a space that connects to the kitchen and living room, and leads outside to the covered loggia.

**Left** | An upper-level secondary bedroom enjoys plenty of light brought in by tall windows and a French door leading to a Juliet balcony. The suite provides a built-in planning desk, dual wardrobe and a private entertainment bar.

**Below Left** | This plan's simplicity is most evident in the living room, dining area and kitchen, where a square arch frames views and defines sight lines from one room to another.

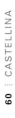

**Above** | A broad square arch offers subtle definition to the family room and kitchen spaces at the front of this plan, expressing an airy aesthetic that is modern and cool. Hand-troweled ceilings, paneled beams and arches and cherry-stained floors create a pleasant ambiance.

# Elements of
# Design

## Bringing The Outdoors In

■ Spacious patio areas in this award-winning townhome village accommodate outdoor rooms that significantly extend the livability of the interiors. The sloped site permits the building clusters to exploit valley views throughout the community, with floor plans oriented toward the rear perimeter. French doors take in the scenery and activate interior spaces with links to open-air verandas, patios and decks. Layered massing and asymmetrical forms permit daylight to enter the homes at oblique angles, creating interplay between the rear edges and streams of light. Rooms are allowed to dissolve into natural settings, infusing these reflections of old-world houses with a modern sense of space. Proportioned to accommodate conversation groups and informal meals, the outdoor rooms are furnishable in size and provide an airy place allied to indoor living areas. Timber beams and wood trellises offer a warm contrast to precast columns and stone floor tiles, contributing to the defining characteristics of the style. A series of brick-lined arches marks the rear perimeter of several plans, framing the views and creating a signature look to the rear elevation.

# The Province

BUILDER: STANDARD PACIFIC HOMES • LOCATION: INDIAN WELLS, CALIFORNIA • PHOTOGRAPHY: ANTHONY GOMEZ

## RESIDENCE FOUR

Classic architecture sets the tone for a desert community at Indian Wells. This Italianate villa reflects Old World traditions, with a recessed paneled entry harbored by a central turret that adds verticality to the single-story elevation. Bone-white plaster set off by wood-trim shutters and window elements hints at an early Mediterranean theme that is reinforced by cupola-like accents and a simple, clay-tiled roof. Airy colonnades and scores of windows open the home to wide views of the desert set against the profile of nearby Eisenhower Mountain. The formal plan progresses from the entry vestibule to a secluded living room, or parlor, through an extensive gallery that opens to the formal dining room and wraps the courtyard perimeter. Natural light brought in by a rear loggia is enhanced by spatial and visual connections to the side courtyard, which contains an inviting deck, pool and fountain. Throughout the home, sight lines draw guests into the public rooms, and help separate the entertainment areas from the quiet owners' retreat and private guest suites.

**Above** | Sculpted cornices and clay-tile roofs reveal the Mediterranean influences of this courtyard design. A decorative vent provides an idiomatic accent above a recessed entry and a series of unmatched windows.

**Below** | The side courtyard brings a sense of serenity that extends beyond the outdoor living area to the public and informal rooms, which wrap the outside space. Elements such as traditional coping of the pool and masonry pavers create an historic ambience.

**Above** | The gourmet kitchen boasts an island and serving counter that invites easy meals and family gatherings. Dark-stained floors and cabinets contrast with créme-colored walls and tile backsplash.

**Below** | A scalloped edge on the sculpted arch offers subtle definition to the space between the family room and kitchen. Carved details set apart the open arrangements of rooms throughout the home, providing separation without interfering with views.

**Above** | Double French doors open an airy master retreat to a private patio and spacious back property, engaging the warm, neutral tones of the interior with great outdoor vistas. Twin windows bring in glimpses of scenery and plenty of natural light.

# The Province

BUILDER: STANDARD PACIFIC HOMES • LOCATION: INDIAN WELLS, CALIFORNIA • PHOTOGRAPHY: ANTHONY GOMEZ

## RESIDENCE FIVE

In an established enclave of single-level residences, the home achieves a resort-style presence, with airy, informal living spaces connected to highly functional outdoor areas. At the street, layered massing shapes an asymmetrical arrangement of the central turret framed by front- and side-facing gables. The sand-colored, weathered-brick exterior conceals an innovative plan that begins with a recessed entry and portico, leading through the side courtyard to create an inviting processional to the formal entry. A secluded casita offers an easy transition from the front property to the patio and pool area, maintaining a vital link to the outdoors. The house is designed around the courtyard and covered patio, wrapping the edges of the outside living space with rows of French doors. Inside, perpendicular galleries take advantage of their ground-level orientation to capture natural light and views of the courtyard. During daylight hours, the shade offered by the covered patio adds a highly desired convenience, allowing casual meals and conversations to be enjoyed in a sheltered environment. On balmy evenings, the open courtyard inspires a deep appreciation of the dry desert climate.

**About The Floor Plan:** This C-shaped plan invites outdoor living, with a portico, courtyard and covered courtyard linking the home to the desert climate that surrounds it. The forward gallery opens to a formal dining room and, through a colonnade, to the family room, kitchen and nook. Oriented toward the rear perimeter and around the side/central courtyard, French doors increase light and circulation throughout the home's interior. Flexible spaces include an optional outdoor kitchen, which may be converted to guest quarters.

## Legend

| | | |
|---|---|---|
| 1 Entry Portal | 9 Kitchen | 17 Exercise Room |
| 2 Casita | 10 Nook | 18 Bedroom Suite |
| 3 Side Courtyard | 11 Hall | 19 Garage |
| 4 Covered Courtyard | 12 Powder Room | 20 Bathroom |
| 5 Entry | 13 Laundry | 21 Outdoor Kitchen |
| 6 Gallery Hall | 14 Retreat | 22 Outdoor Dining |
| 7 Dining Room | 15 Master Bedroom | |
| 8 Family Room | 16 Master Bathroom | |

3,490 SQUARE FEET

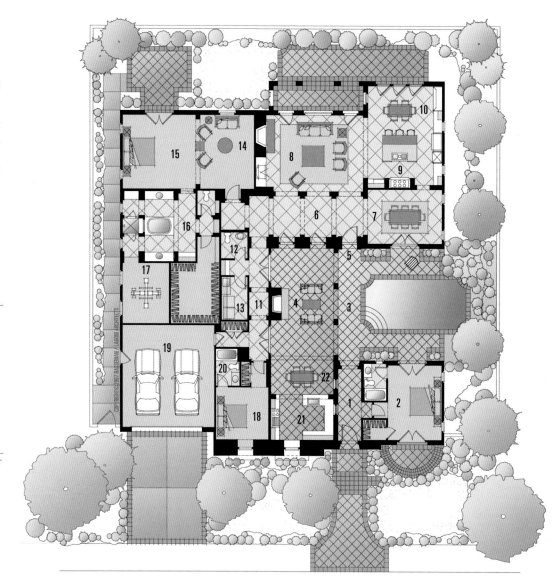

**Right** | Iron brackets and overhanging eaves affirm the Spanish roots of the design. Carriage lights flank a scrolled wrought-iron gate that leads through the portico to the courtyard.

**Above** | Cherry-colored cabinetry enriches a gourmet kitchen featuring a food-preparation island. The family room is arranged to allow family gatherings that include the cook.

**Left** | The side/central courtyard provides an idyllic outdoor environment for gatherings with guests or merely sunbathing. An arcade creates an airy border for the covered patio, and offers a unifying element for the arena. A detailed brick surround enriches the French doors leading to the casita.

**Above** | From the tiled entry hall, a series of arches telescopes toward the formal dining room, creating an impressive site line and airy boundary for the great room.

**Below** | A sculpted arch carved with a scalloped edge lends a subtle sense of separation to the master bedroom and the foreground sitting area, which features its own views of the back property.

**Above** | An outdoor fireplace with a masonry surround anchors the covered patio, and offers warmth and ambience to a generous, open-air sitting area overlooking the courtyard.

# Destino at Vellano

BUILDER: SHEA HOMES • LOCATION: CHINO HILLS, CALIFORNIA • PHOTOGRAPHY: LANCE GORDON

## THE COMMUNITY

Compatible arrangements of exterior styles organized on sloping lots create a village-like environment in this carefully planned neighborhood. Varying lot sizes honor the terrain, offering unique elevations at the streetscape. Authentic European themes employ stone, brick, tile and sun-washed hues to achieve harmony with the rural setting. Central courtyards create processional approaches to the formal entries of the homes. Arcaded galleries open the interiors to views and natural light, with key rooms positioned at the rear perimeters, where walls of glass and French doors connect the homes to their surroundings. Decks and covered patios enrich each plan's relationship to the outdoors.

**Above Right** | A central courtyard provides a generous outdoor living area with a fireplace and spatially connects the home and casita.

**Right** | A main-level master bedroom overlooks its hilly surroundings, and enjoys access to a covered patio shared with the breakfast room.

**Below Right** | In this single-level plan, a sculpted arch provides subtle definition to an open arrangement of the great room and kitchen.

# The Cortile Collection at The Bridges

BUILDER: HCC INVESTORS/LENNAR COMMUNITIES • LOCATION: RANCHO SANTA FE, CALIFORNIA • PHOTOGRAPHY: ERIC FIGGE

## RESIDENCE FOUR

Inspired by earlier renaissance styles, this formal Italian villa pairs a refined two-story stucco elevation with a square-pier entry. Flanked by a single-level wing, the forward vertical structure echoes the classic architectural proportions of a gentler era. Sited in a walkable community with an array of neighboring Tuscan-style estates, the home's grand symmetry conveys a street presence that is urban yet pedestrian-friendly, with the three-car garage placed at the side to preserve the vitality of the public view. As the plan unfolds, it is designed to allow spaces to take on a more relaxed scale, creating a balance that is straight-forward yet stately. Beyond the front of this home, a side courtyard intentionally penetrates the footprint, increasing light and air at the core of the interior. The same attention to design is manifested around the elevation: at the rear perimeter, a protected loggia acts to soften the transition between the living area and the open back property. Designed to provide a sequential experience from the entry to the rear yard, the plan interposes a high-volume public zone with vistas and sightlines that extend toward the informal wing. The fluid progression of the home from the well-defined forward rooms to the open dimensions of the rear

**Above** | Panels of glass and French doors orient the casual living spaces at the back of the house toward views of the property and a sense of the outdoors. The earthy palette repeats the warm tones of Italian villas, while the wrought-iron balustrade is a characteristic elaboration of the style.

living spaces follows a design pattern prescribed for California, where a year-round climate calls for view-oriented informal zones. The spacious side courtyard, loggia, balcony and deck all enhance outdoor living experiences and invite an enjoyment of nature into the home. The plan integrates an elegant yet relaxed interior environment with convertible options that add flexibility: a main-level guest suite or home office, a walk-in entertainment bar or servery, and a secluded morning room that acts as an informal gathering area. Architectural details such as open beams, warm colors and simple square arches dominate the family room and kitchen. A book loft, which wraps the library, adds a sense of volume and space to the entire front of the home—another element of formality borrowed from centuries past.

**About The Floor Plan:** Formal rooms flank the entry of this well-scaled traditional plan. Under the library's 20-foot ceiling, an auxiliary staircase leads to an open book loft that adds a greater sense of space and light. Anchored by a central foyer, the gallery links the dining room with the courtyard via French doors, creating a connection with the outside space. A secluded master suite complements the upper-level sleeping quarters, and opens to a private deck.

## Legend

| | | |
|---|---|---|
| 1 Entry | 9 Side Courtyard | 17 Loggia |
| 2 Living Room | 10 Butler's Pantry | 18 Garage |
| 3 Music Room | 11 Laundry | 19 Book Loft |
| 4 Powder Room | 12 Wine Storage | 20 Bedroom |
| 5 Guest Bedroom | 13 Walk-in Pantry | 21 Master Bedroom |
| 6 Bathroom | 14 Morning Room | 22 Master Bathroom |
| 7 Dining Room | 15 Kitchen | 23 Deck/Balcony |
| 8 Gallery Hall | 16 Family Room | |

5,234 SQUARE FEET

**Second Floor**

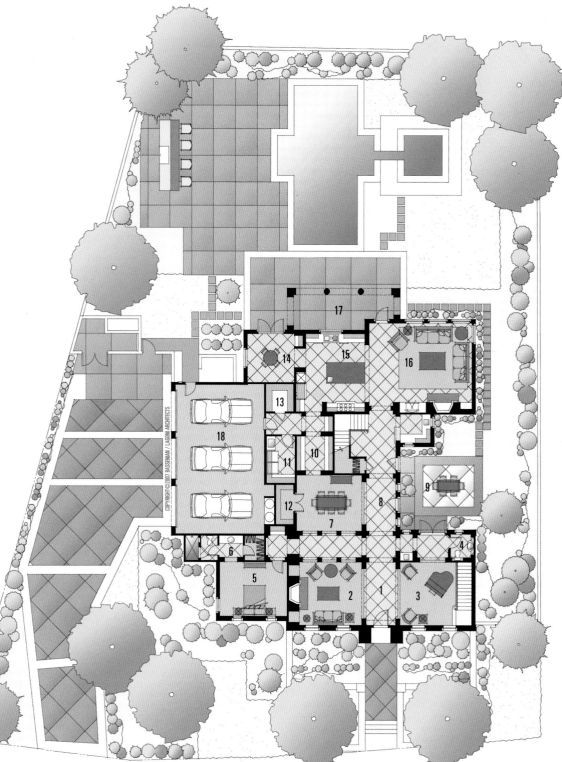

**Opposite Page** | Dual French doors open to the side courtyard, linking the alfresco living area to the formal dining room and to the stair hall, which adjoins a servery and wet bar. To the left, the space leads to the library and loft via a service hall.

**Above** | Framed by a colonnade of arches and anchored by a massive mantel and surround, the living room affirms the formality of the front of the plan. Rustic ceiling beams and glass-paneled cabinet doors give the room a desired connection to history.

**Above** | Paneled cream-colored cabinetry and pale leaf-green walls reinforce the soft interior motifs of the home in a kitchen designed for family gatherings as well as traditional occasions. The food-prep area adjoins a hall and butler's pantry that links to the formal dining room.

# Elements of
# Design

## Classic Is Timeless

■ Pre-cast trim and corner elements drawn from an authentic European vocabulary contribute to this revival of Italian Renaissance style. Rows of pedimented windows flank the entry, suggesting a formality borrowed from later interpretations of the theme. Crafted brackets and detailed eaves dominate the cornice line beneath the low-pitched hipped roof, characteristic of Mediterranean design. Tonal variations in the stucco elevation enhance subtle changes of color and texture in the intentionally uneven rows of terracotta roof tiles. Significant embellishments, such as the Juliet balcony and wrought-iron balustrade above the entry, induce a pristine past with few concessions made to the passage of time. Shutters and surrounds on rows of windows replicate period features. Natural materials bestow a vintage character on the classic symmetry of the façade, which achieves visual fusion with the prevalent, more rustic, Tuscan architecture that shapes the community. True to the classic theme of the home, formal rooms are presented at the front of the floor plan, with the public areas open to the entry—an architectural element that has endured the test of time. Light is drawn into the house at the courtyard via the gallery, which serves as an axial element upstairs as well as downstairs, allowing myriad views of the outside space. Stacked architecture at the center and to the back of the plan also permits increased circulation and flow, and a sequential unfolding of the house on both levels.

# The Lakes

BUILDER: LENNAR • LOCATION: RANCHO SANTA FE, CALIFORNIA
PHOTOGRAPHY: ERIC FIGGE

## THE COMMUNITY

The Spanish colonial homes of The Lakes capture the spirit of Hollywood's Golden Era of architecture. Made popular by the works of such celebrated architects as George Washington Smith, Lilian Jenette Rice and Wallace Neff, these homes exhibit smooth, simple façades and balanced proportions that borrow heavily from Early California vernacular. The elevations employ a diverse range of forms, massing and heritage details to shape this community's rich street scene. Based on centuries-old Andalusian structures, the homes feature private courtyards that create harmony between interior spaces and the natural environment. Loggias, balconies and decks unite the rooms with their surroundings and effect sunny transitions to the enclosed gardens, courtyards and patios.

**Above** | Framed by a parabolic arch, the forecourt provides an inviting processional to the formal entry. A row of clerestory windows, underscored by a barrel-tile roof, helps define the forward loggia.

**Opposite Page Above** | A large, mullion window in the formal dining room brings in picturesque views of the San Dieguito River Valley. The archway to the rear of the room leads through a butler's pantry to the prep kitchen.

**Opposite Page Center** | With pure geometric forms, this Spanish Colonial Revival elevation creates an elegant composite of modern and heritage elements. A casita flanks the entry portico, topped by a deck and upper-level studio.

**Opposite Page Below** | A full complement of shed, hipped and cross-gabled rooflines defines this rear elevation, and authenticates the spirit of the plan. French doors line the loggia, and link the great room with views of the deck and pool.

**Above** | A graceful arcade and loggia add dimension to this rear elevation, which is further extended by a large patio with pool and decorative fountain. The asymmetry of the gables and stepped massing create natural rhythms that relate the house to its site.

**Opposite Page Above** | An informal arrangement of the great room and kitchen permits impromptu gatherings and conversation between guests and family. A simple square arch defines the separation between the food-preparation area and nook.

**Opposite Page Below** | Secluded to the side of the plan, the office is accessed from the entry foyer through an open archway. Windows allow abundant natural light to penetrate from the covered loggia and forecourt.

# Wine Country Residence

## AT PASO ROBLES

BUILDER: WOODY WOODRUFF CONSTRUCTION CO. • LOCATION: PASO ROBLES, CALIFORNIA • PHOTOGRAPHY: ERIC FIGGE

Quiet integrations of line and space play against the many moods of the sky in this modernist elevation, poised on the crest of a hill overlooking the coastal mountains of central California. Expressing native elements in a varied, intricate arrangement, the house retains a simple vocabulary of materials. Rugged fieldstone walls, heavy timber beams, and clay-tiled roofs replicate the rustic details of early pueblo dwellings, while parapets and a curved wall are converted to the bold, simple forms and intense colors of a contemporary exterior. Without front, side, or rear property-line constraints, the design rests organically on the hilltop, deploying crisp lines and smooth planes of color to effect unity with its surroundings. Broken into a collection of smaller buildings, the plan captures the simplicity of its setting with a series of geometric forms—rectangles and shed roofs—connected by a single curved axis. The approach to the entry is anchored by a sculpted terracotta-colored cylinder that offers contrast with the linear forms. Massive walls interlinked with small garden courtyards create transitions via sliding glass doors—portals that allow great fingers of light to penetrate the building forms. Oriented toward the sunset, the primary rooms step into the landscape and absorb views that on clear days extend for miles.

**About The Floor Plan** | A complex of buildings is linked by a curved axis that unifies the structure. Although the plan is not fully revealed at the entry, the entrance court immediately establishes a sense of logic, and the central gallery continues this organization from building to building through continual reference to the courtyards.

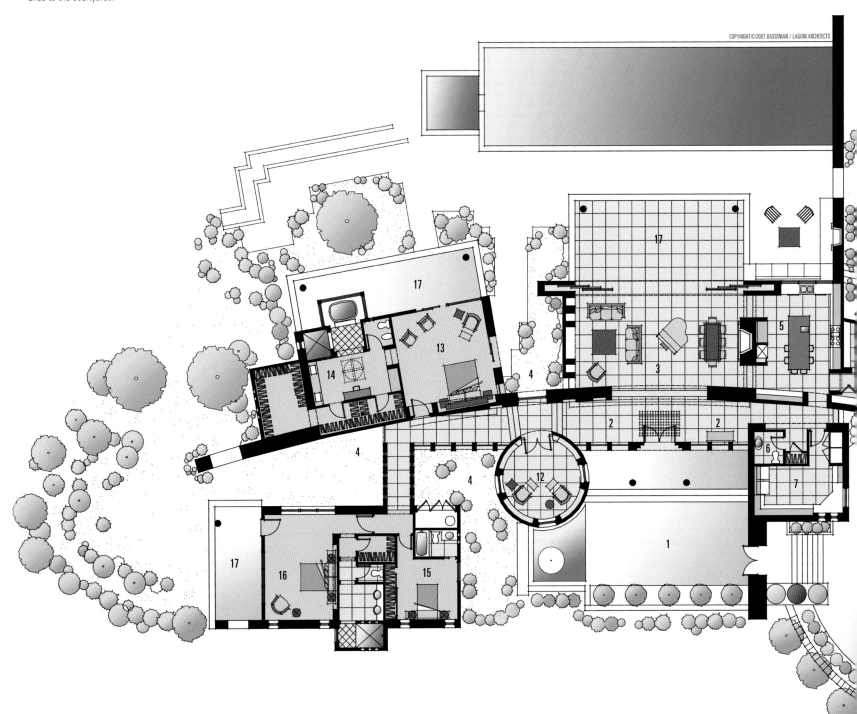

**Previous Page** | A stacked-fieldstone wall seems to rise from the rocky outcroppings that line the entry courtyard. House and garden are animated by brightly colored art balls—playful abstract sculptures designed to add scale and introduce whimsy at the point of arrival.

**Right** | Configured to capture the site's 360-degree views, the house is expressed in a series of primary forms, each building comprising one "hut" of the village-like cluster. A western orientation captures sunsets at the rear perimeter, and positions the home to overlook the owners' vineyards and a forest of oak groves.

### Legend

| | | |
|---|---|---|
| 1 Entry Courtyard | 7 Laundry/Utility Room | 13 Master Bedroom |
| 2 Central Gallery Hall | 8 Storage | 14 Master Bathroom |
| 3 Great Room | 9 Mud Room | 15 Bedroom |
| 4 Courtyard | 10 Pool Bathroom | 16 Guest Suite |
| 5 Kitchen | 11 Garage | 17 Covered Terrace |
| 6 Powder Room | 12 Library | 18 Equipment Area |

4,526 SQUARE FEET

**Above** | Receding glass doors offer a seamless integration with the outdoors between the indoor living area and the terrace. Bold forms create modern expressions that counter the warm textures of tile and wood.

**Right** | Concrete columns, steel beams and overhanging eaves define the boundaries of the sheltered outdoor living spaces. Multi-levels of Canterra stone allow ample spaces for open-air conversation groups, and create an engaging interplay with the rocky terrain.

**Above** | A triple-window view of the side property infuses the southern-most guest suite with a sense of nature. Wood ceiling panels conceal lighting fixtures that indirectly add a sense of warmth and vitality to the room.

**Right** | In the great room, views of the distant horizon mingle with elements of a modernist vocabulary. Pure shapes and sweeping lines unite the primary living space with an eloquent assemblage of light.

**Above** | Geometric forms pervade the primary rooms of the house, subdued by a mix of rustic and urbane materials. Raw timber beams contradict an intricate neon wall sculpture that adds splashes of sapphire, chartreuse and amethyst to the room's neutral palette.

**Opposite Page** | Harbored within the cylinder, the library offers a dramatic vista of the rolling hills to the east through a tall glass portal that blurs the boundary between indoors and out.

**Above** | Characterized by honest, unornamented materials, the master bedroom achieves integrity with its surroundings via glass portals that open to a garden courtyard.

**Right** | Beyond the cloud-white walls of the master bath, hilly stretches of oak groves and vineyards roll toward the coastal mountains—a view that becomes an integral part of the architecture and aesthetic of the home.

**Above** | The house is centered around the gallery, a curved axis which forms a passageway connecting the main living areas and organizing the flow and circulation of the home. Among the sculptures that line the hall, two wicker balls announce the entrance to the library.

# Elements of
# Design

## Blending With The Environment

■ Like a village on the hilltop, the house responds to the site with a simple fusion of contrasting forms and minimalist details that engage the character of the rural surroundings. The individual qualities of each building are respected with organized rhythms of scenery that promote flow to the outside spaces. Spun with the basic architectural materials of steel, concrete, wood and plaster, the design conveys a sense of the outdoors through the use of stone and other natural elements on the inside. Bold forms that reach beyond the roofline are designed to create a dialogue between land and sky, and accentuate the exterior shapes. Garden spaces between the buildings are carefully located to permit daylight and glimpses of the view via glass window and door panels. Structural lines designed to obey the slope of the site create a contemporary framework for the strong colors and varied textures of wood and tile, softening the scale of the home. In a land of contrasts, the home exhibits versatility in its integrations of spatial, structural, and utility elements, and above all, its natural link to the surrounding environment.

# Three-65 at Victoria Gardens

BUILDER: SHEA HOMES • LOCATION: RANCHO CUCAMONGA, CALIFORNIA • PHOTOGRAPHY: WILL HARE, JR.

An upscale collection of flats and townhomes, this neighborhood of attached residences represents a modern composite of Prairie architecture. Horizontal lines and low-pitched, hipped roofs typify the vernacular, adapted here to a compact urban scale suited to a mixed-use community. Layered surfaces and four-sided architecture create interest on the public and private sides of the buildings. Below the roof line, mullion patterns, which are inherent to Prairie and Bungalow styles, give emphasis to groupings of windows that dominate the elevations. Massive square piers that define outdoor living areas—a universal feature of this architecture—break the symmetry of the upper-level structures. Below the decks, large porches encased in red brick with arched, hearth-style openings symbolize the broad, flat chimneys of this vernacular. A third-story loft in one of four floor plans creates a tower room on one end of the building, adding asymmetrical elements to the roof planes.

**Above** | Interior windows lining an upper-level master suite overlook the living room. Light pours into the space through four clerestory windows, which add to the daylight brought in by a main-level picture window.

**Above Right** | In the kitchen, a peninsular counter doubles as a pass-through to a flexible space in the living area that has been converted to the dining room. The rectilinear pattern of the flooring echoes the horizontal bands and subtle dark-light geometry that typify the style.

**Below Right** | Vibrant combinations of brick, masonry and clap-board siding define the horizontal planes of the building. Wrought-iron rails and the use of brick and other materials lend a Prairie identity to the plan.

# Altamura

BUILDER: WILLIAM LYON HOMES  •  LOCATION: LAGUNA HILLS, CALIFORNIA  •  PHOTOGRAPHY: ERIC FIGGE

## RESIDENCE THREE

Nested high in the foothills at Nellie Gail Ranch, this clapboard-and-brick façade conceals an engaging 21st-century courtyard plan that adds light to the interior with an array of outdoor spaces. Dual porches, including one that wraps around a flexible home office or library, highlight the traditional East Coast exterior, which positions the swing garage away from the public view to create a pedestrian-friendly approach to the home. Designed to blend with the streetscape of the twenty-year-old neighborhood, this new home preserves the heritage of the region while integrating a modern, multi-function court to enhance the flexibility and flow of the plan. Inside, the entry foyer yields to a main gallery that permits access to both the covered and open areas of the central court, pro-

viding an airy boundary for the dining room and stair hall. Traditional rooms are linked by the corridor, which floods the spaces with natural light from the courtyard via a series of French doors. Great views abide throughout the plan, and the home's relationship with the courtyard does more than expand the rooms. Designed to permit maximum light into the home, the perimeter edges forward and back, creating layers of spaces that transition from indoors to out. The living room employs tall windows to bring in a sense of the outdoors, and even the secluded library enjoys a connection to nature, wrapped by a spacious front porch. Upstairs, the master suite stretches across the width of the plan, providing access to decks on both sides and permitting light to enter the home.

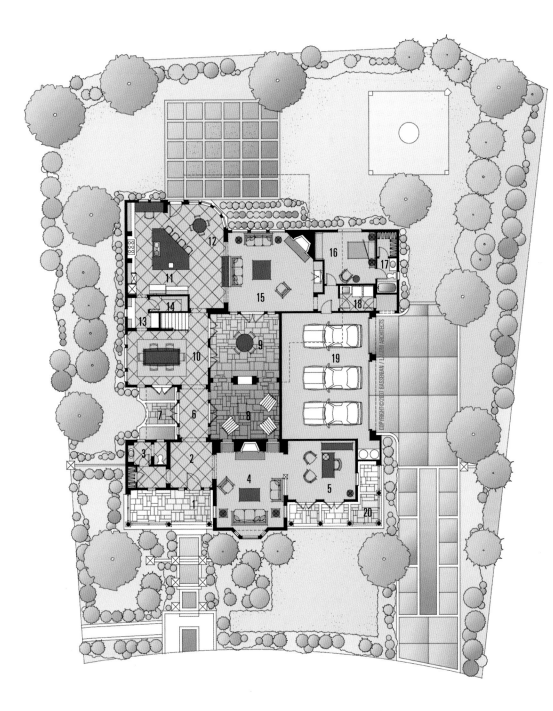

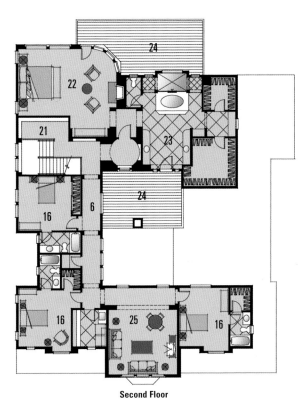

**Second Floor**

## Legend

| | | |
|---|---|---|
| 1 Entry Porch | 10 Dining Room | 19 Garage |
| 2 Entry | 11 Kitchen | 20 Porch |
| 3 Powder Room | 12 Nook | 21 Library/Loft |
| 4 Living Room | 13 Butler's Pantry | 22 Master Bedroom |
| 5 Home Office/Library | 14 Walk-in Pantry | 23 Master Bathroom |
| 6 Gallery Hall | 15 Family Room | 24 Deck/Balcony |
| 7 Side Courtyard | 16 Bedroom | 25 Game Room |
| 8 Central Courtyard | 17 Bathroom | |
| 9 Covered Courtyard | 18 Laundry | |

5,776 SQUARE FEET

**Opposite Page** | Cloud-white clapboard siding sets off a central brick gable on a classic Northeastern elevation configured with broad outdoor spaces. An intimate sitting area softens the transition to the street and invites interactions with passers-by.

**Previous Page** | In the central courtyard, sculpted arches set in a brick wall frame a dual-sided fireplace, repeating the exterior materials of the home. A master deck overlooks the sitting area, while a covered patio behind the courtyard offers space for outdoor meals sheltered from the sun.

# Foxfield

BUILDER: PARDEE HOMES  •  LOCATION: YORBA LINDA, CALIFORNIA  •  PHOTOGRAPHY: JEFF SMITH

## RESIDENCE THREE

More cutting edge than convention, this courtyard home integrates a compelling mix of authentic materials with intuitive yet intellectual design. From the street, the home appears carved from the heart of Americana: a traditional exterior of classic clapboard siding—the color of fresh cream—enriched by a grey tile roof and a gable of decorative stone. Authentic details such as double-hung sashes, red-brick lintels and an upper-level balustrade reinforce the rural vocabulary, retuned to an appealing urban scale. The sheltered porch sets off a varied roofline that mimics the terraced terrain and helps to unite the plan with its hillside location. Inside, the plan offers a highly functional, 21st-century character with multiple living options and playful, unexpected spaces that heighten the versatility of the home. The side-court plan permits an exceptional degree of customization. Just off the entry, a bedroom suite converts to a home office, while the supersized family room may be split to incorporate a separate den or guest suite; upstairs, a wide loft might become Bedroom Five. An example of a well-organized home, the highly functional design offers a great sense of space, with intimate links to the outdoors. The open living and dining room arrangement grants a sweeping view of the central stairwell and loft, adding volume and dimension to the core of the home. French doors open the dining room to the side courtyard, a secluded, informal setting that supplements the large rear yard. Natural light is invited deep into the plan, permitting many opportunities for living out-of-doors.

**Previous Page Above** | The neat-as-a-pin traditional exterior is accentuated by white clapboard siding, decorative stone and grey roof tiles. A balcony from the upstairs family room adds detail to the front-facing gable over the garage.

**Previous Page Below** | A wide balcony accessible from the owners' suite overlooks a back property designed for outdoor living, while French doors and a trio of windows bring in natural light to the supersized family room. Both the strategically placed patio and spacious backyard, located conveniently off the casual zone, offer splendid areas for open-air meals and outdoor entertaining.

**Above** | Steps at the landing harbor a book loft brightened by a wide archway and views of the side property. Hardwood floors mingle with plush carpeting on the upper level, with the far wing designated as living and sleeping spaces for children.

**Left** | Contemporary colors play counterpoint to stained maple handrails and a hardwood floor in the public realm. The stairwell and loft present sweeping interior vistas above the formal dining room, enhanced by two-level volume and views to the side courtyard.

**Legend**

| | | |
|---|---|---|
| 1 Entry | 7 Kitchen | 13 Bedroom |
| 2 Guest Bedroom | 8 Nook | 14 Laundry |
| 3 Bathroom | 9 Family Room | 15 Study Area |
| 4 Living Room | 10 Game Room | 16 Master Bedroom |
| 5 Dining Room | 11 Garage | 17 Master Bathroom |
| 6 Side Courtyard | 12 Library/Loft | 18 Deck Balcony |

3,608 SQUARE FEET

**Second Floor**

**About The Floor Plan:** Oriented toward a multigenerational market, the courtyard plan achieves the targeted size of nearly 4,000 square feet, set in an articulated footprint on an elevated site. Room options expand the function of both upper and lower levels, with a high bed and bath count, and alternatives that include such luxe amenities as a game room and book loft. Outdoor spaces are notched into the periphery to the side and rear of the plan, with a master deck above that overlooks the fairway.

# Montanez at Covenant Hills

BUILDER: CENTEX HOMES • LOCATION: LADERA RANCH, CALIFORNIA • PHOTOGRAPHY: ANTHONY GOMEZ

## RESIDENCE ONE

Set among the hills of San Juan Capistrano, this English Country elevation presents a series of prominent overlapping gables and steeply pitched rooflines, enriched by a rustic blend of brick and stucco. Varied eave lines, exposed rafter tails and recessed windows establish today's interpretation of a 19th-century Tudor-style cottage in an upscale community of eclectic styles. Versatile areas on the main floor include an airy, well-lit dining room that relates closely to the courtyard via a covered loggia. An adjoining butler's pantry, featuring an optional sink and wine cooler, leads to a dramatic space formed by an open arrangement of the morning room, kitchen and great room. A series of French doors along the rear perimeter brings in plenty of natural light and provides access to the back property, an inviting space that complements the function of the central court.

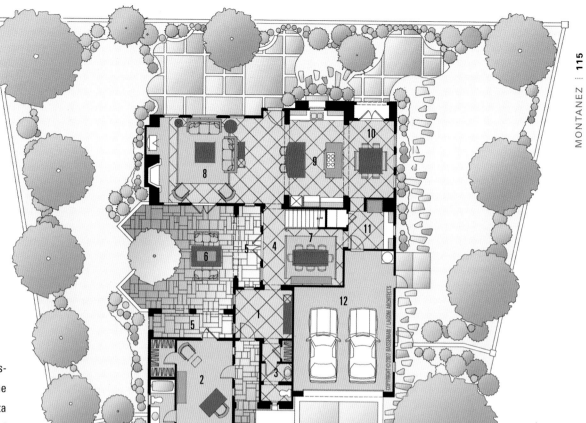

**About The Floor Plan:** Designed to create a processional experience from the sidewalk to the foyer, the plan unfolds in two directions. To the left, a casita offers private access for guests via the entry portal and an independent link to the central courtyard through a rear French door. Directly ahead, a traditional foyer supported by a powder room and a coat closet establishes the formality of the home and leads to a sequence of spaces activated by sunlight from the side courtyard. Upstairs, the master retreat is extended by a hall leading to a wide tech center designed for computers and homework.

## Legend

| | | |
|---|---|---|
| 1 Entry Foyer | 8 Family Room | 15 Study Area |
| 2 Casita | 9 Kitchen | 16 Bedroom |
| 3 Powder Room | 10 Morning Room | 17 Bathroom |
| 4 Hall | 11 Butler's Pantry | 18 Master Bedroom |
| 5 Covered Courtyard | 12 Garage | 19 Master Bathroom |
| 6 Side Courtyard | 13 Gallery Hall | |
| 7 Dining Room | 14 Laundry | |

3,846 SQUARE FEET

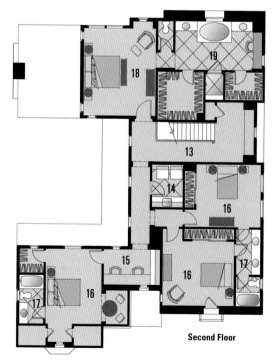

**Second Floor**

**Above** | The formal dining room borrows light from the covered side courtyard, expanding the visual dimensions of the home without intruding on the tranquil facets of the outdoor space.

**Above** | A memorable kitchen results from the creation of dual islands: one designed to host informal meals and the other dedicated as a cook station. The space is intentionally scaled to foster intimate family gatherings yet boasts the capacity to serve a crowd.

# Montanez at Covenant Hills

BUILDER: CENTEX HOMES • LOCATION: LADERA RANCH, CALIFORNIA • PHOTOGRAPHY: ANTHONY GOMEZ

### RESIDENCE THREE

Infused with a sense of the outdoors, this courtyard home boasts wide views of the Capistrano hills and opens to a spacious courtyard at its core. Classical elements are present in the clean lines of the clapboard elevation: square columns and balustrades evoke the grace and beauty of Seaboard Colonial houses. Reflective of the geometry of seaside vernaculars, the pure forms of the entry portico capture the tranquility of a breezy waterfront cottage. From the street, a sense of informality reinforces the coastal origins of the plan. A three-car garage is set back from the street and intentionally de-emphasized, while a deep front porch offers outdoor living and friendship to its neighbors. Inside, a time-honored arrangement of the foyer and living room leads to a grand stair hall and a formal dining room with links to the courtyard. Adjacent to the casual living area, the courtyard serves multiple functions, not the least of which is to provide a splendid outdoor retreat.

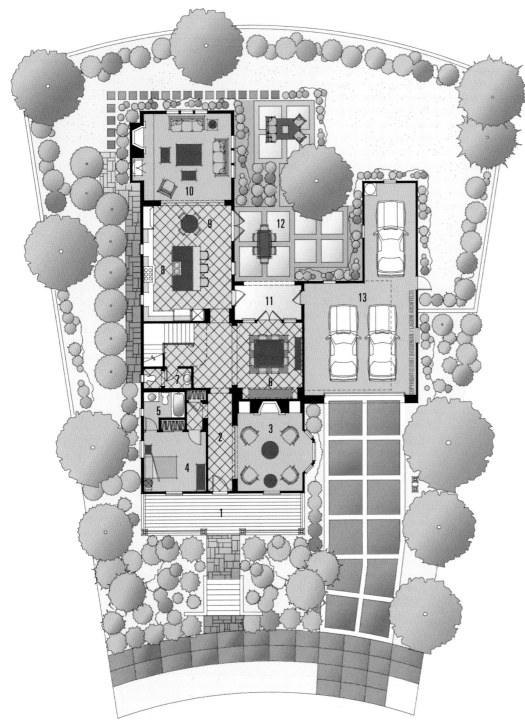

**Second Floor**

### Legend

| | | |
|---|---|---|
| 1 Entry Porch | 8 Kitchen | 15 Bedroom |
| 2 Entry | 9 Nook | 16 Master Bedroom |
| 3 Living Room | 10 Family Room | 17 Master Bathroom |
| 4 Guest Bedroom | 11 Covered Courtyard | 18 Veranda |
| 5 Bathroom | 12 Rear Courtyard | 19 Laundry |
| 6 Dining Room | 13 Garage | 20 Deck/Balcony |
| 7 Powder Room | 14 Media Room | |

3,730 SQUARE FEET

**About The Floor Plan:** Rooms positioned at the front of the plan exhibit the proportions necessary to achieve an eye-pleasing balance between the public and private sectors of the home. French doors connect the morning nook to the rear courtyard, while triple-window views of the space enrich the family room. Upstairs, a cluster of flexible spaces offers a series of links to the outdoors: a convertible bonus room provides access to a balcony linked to the master suite. Bedroom Two enjoys a private deck, while the larger bedroom suites share the veranda and views of the front property.

**Previous Page** | A sleek metal pavilion adds dimension and definition to the rear courtyard and harbors an intimate outdoor sitting area. Sight lines extend through an informal alfresco eating area and the covered courtyard to the formal dining room.

**Opposite Page** | An inviting extension of the upper floor plan, the veranda inspires fidelity to outdoor living, the enjoyment of fresh air and a love of the natural environment. A welcome counterpart to the central courtyard, this space offers a place of repose for the owners and their guests.

**Above** | Located to the rear of the plan, the family room extends the dramatic open space of the nook and kitchen. Surrounded by windows, the casual living area creates an airy retreat for guests and family, and links to the courtyard through the nook.

**Above** | Natural light filters through French doors from the courtyard to the morning nook and kitchen, illuminating cloud-white cabinetry and sleek 21st-century appliances, and amplifying the circulation of the private realm.

# Front Street

BUILDER: **STANDARD PACIFIC HOMES** • LOCATION: **LADERA RANCH, CALIFORNIA** • PHOTOGRAPHY: **LANCE GORDON**

## RESIDENCE TWO

One of California's most innovative neighborhoods, Front Street represents a practical alternative to suburban living, with a singular collection of live/work designs. A quadrant of 22 houses, the community is zoned for both commercial and residential use and presents a broad vocabulary of exterior styles that include Charleston-inspired Colonials, Monterey Haciendas and Nantucket Cape Cods. Wound with a network of pedestrian trails and paseos, the community effectively promotes a flourish of private businesses in an environment that also encourages bicycling, hiking and walking. Each plan accommodates a service-based commercial enterprise, with the placement of the work-at-home area to the front or rear, depending on the type of business. Professionals that require public interaction, such as an attorney or interior designer, benefit from a formal, street-facing entry; trades that focus on delivery-based services utilize the private loops and alleys that feed the alternate "front" doors. With the public's propensity to work at home, the project provides a ground-breaking view of live-work design, paving the way for the next great step in suburban evolution.

# Elements of
# Design

## A Live/Work Concept

**Above** | Pre-wired for intelligent technology, the office space at the mezzanine (photo left) works as hard as the commercial area below (photo right). Upper-level views offer a corner-office ambience that enhances the private work area of the home.

**Previous Page** | A seamless approach to the outdoors is evident at the center of the plan, where a single French door expands the family's living space to a side courtyard. The loggia shelters the alfresco dining area from the sun, and leads into the work studio through a private side door.

**Opposite Page Right** | The rear alley entrance to the work space—the other "front door"—is as ordered and elegant as the formal streetside entrance to the home.

■ The aim: to create a house plus an office not a house that merely includes an office. The outcome: a home that delivers all of the desirable living spaces plus a private office with an effective commercial space that fits perfectly into its suburban surroundings. In refining and formalizing a practical and stylish live/work unit, necessary design distinctions emerged both in the plan forms and in the floor plan. Clearly distinguishing the residential entry to the home from the business entrance – while preserving a unified architectural character – dictated a seamless approach to the interior and outside living spaces. Creating a multi-level office space with a private-lane entrance to the rear of the plan segregates the business function and carries the Charleston-inspired, Plantation-style architecture around the home. Scaled columns, shuttered windows and clapboard siding evoke a 20th-century seaside manor, providing definition to the rear entrance. The design

3,213 SQUARE FEET

**Second Floor**

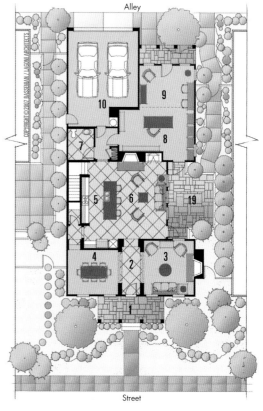

offers approximately 3,213 square feet, with nearly 700 square feet dedicated to the work area. Formal rooms placed to the front of the plan lead to an open arrangement of the family room and kitchen at the center, providing a transition to the work zone. Living areas are deftly connected to the whole house, with the work space/studio readily accessible from the residential zone yet not visible. Sightlines are broken by an L-shaped vestibule that subtly links to the business zone, ensuring a vital, intuitive separation of the office and family functions.

# MiraBay

BUILDER: SABAL HOMES OF FLORIDA • LOCATION: APOLLO BEACH, FLORIDA • PHOTOGRAPHY: ROB/HARRIS PRODUCTIONS

## TRADEWIND RESIDENCE

Tucked along the shores of an inlet of Tampa Bay, this Boca Grande home offers an excellent example of Old Florida architecture, capturing views of the water with an authentic coastal character. Horizontal wood siding, box-bay windows and a seamed metal roof are deftly crafted to showcase the authentic features of the home, a classic cross-gabled plan that strikes a balance between past and present. Highly visible from the waterside as well as the street, the elevation conveys the simple massing of the original style enlivened by an intricate notching of outdoor spaces into the front and rear of the footprint. A forecourt creates an inviting approach to a properly subdued entry; the opposing garages are turned in, away from the streetscene, to preserve the aesthetic of the public view. Along the rear perimeter, inside and outside living areas are oriented toward the waterfront—a screened lanai expands the dimensions of the core of the home and complements a starlight deck that opens the upper level to fresh air and views. The central volume contains the public spaces required for living and entertaining, framed by private sectors that lead outdoors. The master-down plan offers several convertible areas—such as the den and loft—as well as a series of playful elements, including a sunlit game room and a mid-level landing that eases the transition between the upper and lower floors.

## Legend

| | | |
|---|---|---|
| 1 Entry Porch | 9 Family Room | 17 Pool Bathroom |
| 2 Entry | 10 Walk-in Pantry | 18 Gallery Hall |
| 3 Living Room | 11 Laundry | 19 Bedroom |
| 4 Dining Room | 12 Master Bedroom | 20 Bathroom |
| 5 Lanai | 13 Retreat | 21 Game Room |
| 6 Home Office | 14 Master Bathroom | 22 Deck/Balcony |
| 7 Kitchen | 15 Study | |
| 8 Nook | 16 Garage | |

4,015 SQUARE FEET

**About The Floor Plan:** The straightforward H-shaped plan allows each area to open visually to the site yet permits privacy. From the foyer, a through-vista encompasses the central living and dining area, lanai and inlet. The informality of the plan is expressed by the open arrangement of rooms. Opposite the family room and kitchen, the master wing runs the full depth of the house and leads to the secondary garage, offering privacy for the owners. Upstairs, a wide loft overlooks the core living area and leads to a game room with access to the deck.

**Above |** A deeply set front porch runs the width of the elevation and establishes the informal tone of the house. Cloud-white Adirondack chairs inspire a sense of well-being in a setting of trim balustrades and robin's-egg-blue clapboard, wrested from the past.

**Second Floor**

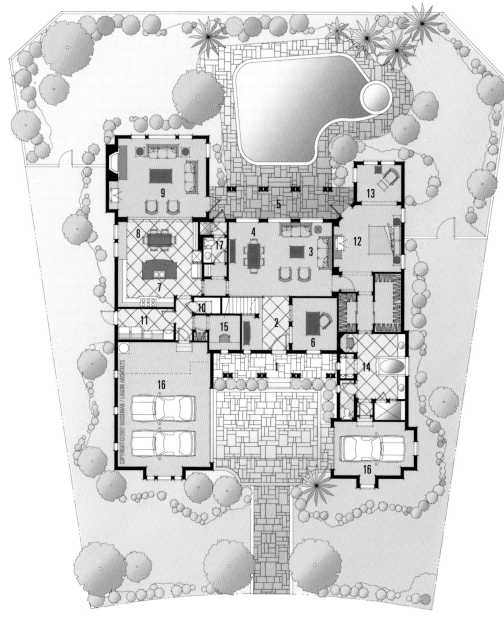

**Above** | Views of the bay and inlet invite repose in the owners' suite, which offers a private door to the pool and lanai. Just beyond the sleeping area, a sitting retreat defines the space with an intimate scale of its own.

**Right** | Oriented toward rear views, the private living and dining areas are infused with an inviting sense of informality that reinforces the seaboard character of the home. An open arrangement of the island kitchen, morning nook and family room allows for interaction between the work space and casual eating area, with plenty of places for people to gather.

# Sutter's Mill

BUILDER: CENTEX HOMES • LOCATION: LADERA RANCH, CALIFORNIA • PHOTOGRAPHY: ERIC FIGGE

## TOWNHOMES

B old tones and cutting-edge lines create an award-winning tour de force in this urban-edge, high-density townhome community. Harbored by the hills of Terramor Village, Sutter's Mill reinforces the overall character of the surrounding area—a green-oriented neighborhood laced with foot trails and walkways—and connects with a network of arroyos, public courtyards and paseos that define the boundaries of the community. Fresh colors enliven elevations influenced by Bay Area row houses, Napa Valley farm buildings and historic mining structures from the Gold Rush era—revived here with striking dimensions and varied composi-

tions. Metal overhangs, cantilevered retreats and high-pitched rooflines integrate the contemporary character of the homes with the angled terrain. Carved into the setting with eco-friendly dimensions, each of the multi-plex clusters offers a quartet of distinctive plans, including a tri-level loft design. The structural purity and sustainability of each unit foster a heightened allegiance to the natural environment, a direction that has been well received by first-time buyers. A vital outcome of this approach was the community's immediate appeal to the intended market of professional singles, young couples and beginning families.

**Above** | An array of building forms reveals connectivity between the structures and their surroundings. The richly varied combination of textures and materials articulates the diversity of organic architecture.

**Right** | Colorful, upper-level retreats project above main-floor entries that address the sidewalk and connect each unit to the public realm.

**Right** | The turret harbors a loft retreat designed for the owners' repose. Layered massing and varied rooflines break up the scale and architectural components of the multi-plex clusters.

**Opposite Page:** A new concept in attached design, this high-density community features clusters of two- and three-level townhomes with pedestrian-friendly approaches and rear-loaded, direct-connect garages accessible via internal alleyways. Steeply angled rooflines and layered building forms create an informal aesthetic that is enriched with fresh combinations of lively colors. Materials such as steel-hung metal awnings and corrugated siding contrast with pure forms of wood and metal, and twist tradition toward an agrarian variation.

# Elements of
# Design

## Fresh Colors & Eco-Sensitive Materials

■ A showcase of four-sided architecture, Sutter's Mill conveys a strong aesthetic by embracing the concept of livable, human-scaled design. Recognized with a national Best in American Living Award, a Gold Nugget for Best Attached Project, and numerous regional honors, the community is also known as a model for sustainable design. Within a green-oriented village, the homes provide a high level of energy-efficiency and sound ecological principles. Multi-layered elevations in vivid yet weathered tones mix stucco, wood and steel in innovative forms, obliques and perpendiculars, with strong lines that tower above surrounding rooftops. Branded "abstract national," the vernacular draws influence from iconic elements of farming and mining structures. Typical agrarian features, such as square turrets, balconies and steeply pitched gables, are reinvented by twisting traditional lines into a contemporized context. Corrugated siding and clapboard—time-honored

vestiges of rural vocabularies—are juxtaposed against high-profile gables and projecting forms, capturing an inventive character that recalls early California dialects. Combining vibrant architecture with a reverence for nature, the townhome community merges bold, contemporary design with eco-sensitive materials. Low-VOC paints and coatings, along with water-based finishes, integrate the splashy palette of hues with a dedication to environmentalism. Steel awnings, exposed beams and commercial cabling serve as counterpoints to raised-panel entry doors—a mere hint of the hand-troweled textures and crafted works inside. The unique mix of massing and materials distinguishes these townhouses from others in the master plan, creating a visually rich, ecologically responsible community.

CHAPTER TWO

ON THE BOARDS

# Umm Al Quwain
# Marina & Golf Resort

BUILDER: EMAAR • LOCATION: UNITED ARAB EMIRATES
WATERCOLOR RENDERINGS: MICHAEL ABBOTT

Scheduled for completion in 2011, this mixed-use development plan for a 1,500-acre site along the Arabian Gulf consists of a destination-resort marina town center, upscale golf course communities, a diverse mix of retail and entertainment facilities, and exclusive recreation areas. With an extensive marina at its core, the plan unfolds with clusters of villas and townhouses on manmade islands linked by navigable waterways. This self-sustaining development partners boutique hotels, waterfront resorts, shops, restaurants and commercial buildings with open beaches, piazzas, parks and hiking trails. The environment embodies a blend of historic and modernist vocabularies. Regular rhythms of surfaces, smooth and textured, paired with atriums and courtyards that emphasize circulation and privacy, counter classical elements with contemporary themes. A primary focus on scale and the careful placement of mixed-use buildings protects the live/work ethos, while natural materials, such as stucco and terracotta, create organic links with the setting.

# Al Khobar Lakes
# Retail Center

BUILDER: EMAAR • LOCATION: SAUDI ARABIA

The Al Khobar Lakes Retail Center is part of a master-planned community located in Saudi Arabia near the Arabian Gulf. The Retail Center is strategically positioned adjacent to the intersection of two expressways, creating a community identity while at the same time establishing a destination point for the entire development. The intent of this localized amenity is to become the focal point for social, recreational, and leisure activities for the surrounding region. Visible from a great distance, the Al Khobar Retail Center has been integrated into the regional surroundings by providing a state-of-the-art facility complementing the local architectural character. The center is positioned to respond to the various climactic conditions of the region by supplying shaded areas, natural light to the interior, and operable fenestration for cross-ventilation. Acting as a terminus, the center evokes a strong sense of procession through dramatic entry features, hierarchical spaces, and rich interior textures and materials. The center will create a destination point for day-to-day activities, such as retail shopping, dining, health and day care, as well as areas for contemplation and retreat. The intent of the facility is to establish a location for neighborhood and local interaction and exchange.

NORTH ELEVATION

# Mohali Hills

BUILDER: EMAAR/MGF • LOCATION: CHANDIGARH, INDIA
GRAPHICS: AMP 3D ZONE

Designed for upscale sectors of Chandigarh, a city defined a half-century earlier by LeCorbusier, this neighborhood of homes infuses India's roots with a current aesthetic. Scaled to a landmass of nearly 1,000 acres, clusters of villas and townhomes advance the area's residential ambience to a contemporary model of planned urbanism. Rigid geometry and palettes of neutral colors convey an aesthetic expressed by cubic forms and linear dimensions, with an emphasis on proportion, scale and detail. Single- and multi-family homes, interposed on compact lots, exhibit exteriors with smooth plaster-finished walls, pre-cast concrete coping and decorative parapet caps. Entries to individual homes are designed for maximum impact. Central and side courtyards offer outside living areas, while varied levels of rooftop terraces extend private retreats. Many homes, drawn to accommodate extended families, include thoughtfully positioned stairwells, which permit a conversion to separate living quarters at a future time.

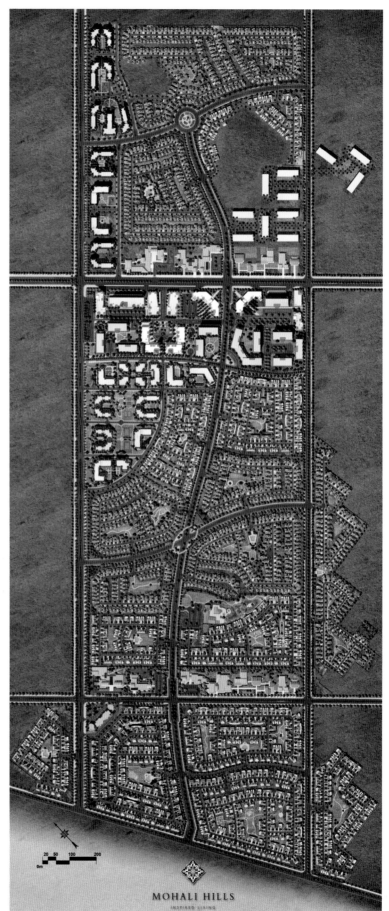

20  50    100         200
0m

MOHALI HILLS
INSPIRED LIVING

# Tinja

BUILDER: EMAAR/MOROCCO • LOCATION: TANGIER, MOROCCO • RENDERING: AMP 3D ZONE

## TOWNHOMES

The architectural vernacular of the Tinja townhomes reflect a contemporary flavor with some influences from traditional motifs. The building cluster is a mixture of four attached homes — each celebrating outdoor living with courtyards, patios, balconies and roof terraces. Each home is designed with layered massing and composed to take full advantage of the nearby ocean and forest. The Tinja master-planned community is located in Tangier, an historic city in the north of Morocco that sits at the western tip of the Strait of Gibraltar where the Mediterranean Sea meets the Atlantic Ocean. This exceptional community fronts on the Atlantic Ocean on the west, a long stretch of native forest to the south and an ecologically rich river estuary to the north. At completion, the 730-acre (295-hectare) Tinja community will offer residents a vibrant town center with hotels, restaurants, a school, a beach club house, a sports facility and parks and lakes. Multiple residential offerings will include luxury villas, apartments (for-sale flats) and townhomes.

# Luxury Villas
## East OCT

BUILDER: OVERSEAS CHINA TOWN CO., LTD. • LOCATION: SHENZHEN, CHINA
GRAPHICS: ARCHIWOOD DESIGN DEVELOPMENT

A short drive from Shenzhen—China's center of foreign investment and one of the fastest growing cities in the world—this corporate retreat will offer repose for business executives in a secluded mountainside setting. Amid a landscape dotted with farms and lakes, the resort-style villa employs North American lodge architecture to deepen the rural character of a contemporary elevation that links closely with the outdoors. Hipped rooflines and overhanging eaves reinforce the clean simplicity of the façade's wide, horizontal layers, evoking elements of Prairie design. Decorative casement windows and sets of double French doors establish lines of symmetry supported by fieldstone and masonry piers. The plan comprises a network of rooms on four levels, which fully engage the site as the house progresses from one level to the next. Octagonal stairwells venture beyond the footprint, creating exterior paths between floors. The design reveals itself gradually, with elements of discovery planned for each space: a formal entry opens to a gallery that leads past a trio of formal spaces—a vaulted living room framed by a library and meeting room—toward a circular terminus and vectored wing that harbors the common areas, including a rustic dining hall.

# Urban Infill Community

LOCATION: CALIFORNIA • RENDERING: MILO OLEA

M I X E D - U S E

A mixed-use development, this plaza provides a retail center at ground level and spacious residential flats throughout the upper floors. With a unique corner identity, the contemporary structure energizes the street with a lively palette of colors and sculpted forms. The forward-thinking residences include such features as two master suites and private balconies.

# Annotated Projects List

**Altamura**
Residence Three
Laguna Hills, California
2003
Pages 106-109

*Bassenian/Lagoni Architects Team:*
*Designers:* Dave Pockett,
 Mike Pilarski
*Project Managers:* Sophia Braverman,
 John Oravetz

*Builder:* William Lyon Homes
*Builder Executive in Charge of Design:*
 Tom Mitchell
*Landscape Architect:* Urban Arena
*Interior Designer:* Design Tec Interiors
*Structural Engineer:* Performance Plus
 Engineering

*Photographer:* Eric Figge

*Awards:*
Best in American Living Awards 2004
 Home of the Year
National Sales & Marketing Awards 2004
 Silver Award
Gold Nuggets 2004
 Grand Award
MAME Awards/Southern California 2003
 Finalist

**Bella Fioré at Lake Las Vegas**
The Community
Henderson, Nevada
2006
Pages 26-31

*Bassenian/Lagoni Architects Team:*
*Designers:* Hans Anderle, Jeff Lake AIA
*Project Manager:* Luis Chavez

*Builder:* Pardee Homes
*Builder Executives in Charge of Design:*
 Bob Clauser, Loren Smets
*Landscape Architect:* SJA
*Interior Designer:* Color Design Art
*Structural Engineer:* Borm Associates

*Photographer:* Eric Figge

*Awards:*
Gold Nuggets 2006
 Merit Award
National Sales & Marketing Awards 2006
 Silver Award

**Casa Bonita del Rio**
Rancho Santa Fe, California
2006
Pages 48-51

*Bassenian/Lagoni Architects Team:*
*Designers:* Kevin Karami, Joe Abrajano
*Project Manager:* Mike Pilarski

*Client:* Lance and Anna Waite
*Landscape Architect:* Gillespie Moody
 Patterson
*Interior Designer:* Design Visions
*Structural Engineer:* Performance Plus

*Photographer:* Eric Figge

*Awards:*
Gold Nuggets 2007
 Merit Award

**Castellina at Covenant Hills**
Ladera Ranch, California
2005
Pages 56-63

*Bassenian/Lagoni Architects Team:*
*Designers:* Dave Kosco AIA,
 Kevin Karami, Joe Abrajano,
 Raffi Agaian
*Project Managers:* Jeff Ganyo,
 Ian Sparks

*Builder:* Centex Homes – Southern
 California Coastal Division
*Builder Executives in Charge of Design:*
 Richard Douglass, Nick Lehnert
*Landscape Architect:* Borthwick Guy
 Bettenhausen
*Interior Designer:* Design Tec Interiors
*Structural Engineer:* Van Dorpe Chou
 Associates

*Photographer:* Eric Figge

*Awards:*
Best in American Living Awards 2005
 Residence 4 – Silver Award
National Sales & Marketing Awards 2005
 Residence 4 – Silver Award
Gold Nuggets 2005
 Attached Project – Merit Award
Gold Nuggets 2006
 Community Site Plan – Merit Award
 Attached Neighborhood – Merit Award
 Community of the Year – Merit Award
MAME Awards/Southern California 2004
 Attached Community of the Year
 Winner

152 :: ANNOTATED PROJECTS LIST

**The Cortile Collection
at The Bridges**
Residence Four
Rancho Santa Fe, California
2004
Pages 76-83

*Bassenian/Lagoni Architects Team:*
*Designers:* Dave Kosco AIA,
Craig Gambill AIA
*Project Manager:* Brian Neves AIA

*Builder:* HCC Investors/Lennar
Communities
*Builder Executive in Charge of Design:*
Tom Martin
*Landscape Architect:* Pinnacle Design
*Interior Designer:* Pacific Dimensions
*Structural Engineer:* Performance Plus
Engineering

*Photographer:* Eric Figge

*Awards:*
Gold Nuggets 2004
Project of the Year – Grand Award
Gold Nuggets 2006
Merit Award
MAME Awards/Southern California 2006
Finalist
SAM Awards 2006 – Winner

**Destino at Vellano**
The Community
Chino Hills, California
2006
Pages 74-75

*Bassenian/Lagoni Architects Team:*
*Designers:* Dave Kosco AIA, Ryan White
*Project Manager:* Jeff Marcotte

*Builder:* Shea Homes
*Builder Executive in Charge of Design:*
Bob Yoder
*Landscape Architect:* Forma Design
*Interior Designer:* Oma Talley Design
*Structural Engineer:* ESI/FME

*Photographer:* Lance Gordon

*Awards:*
Laurel Awards 2006
Best Community – Winner
Residence 2 – Winner
Residences 1, 3 and 4 – Finalists

**Foxfield**
Residence Three
Yorba Linda, California
2005
Pages 110-113

*Bassenian/Lagoni Architects Team:*
*Designers:* John Bigot AIA, Jeff Lake AIA
*Project Manager:* Ian Sparks

*Builder:* Pardee Homes
*Builder Executive in Charge of Design:*
Bob Clauser
*Landscape Architect:* SJA
*Interior Designer:* Color Design Art
*Structural Engineer:* Gouvis Engineering

*Photographer:* Jeff Smith

*Awards:*
ELAN Awards 2005
Detached Community of the Year
Finalist

**Front Street**
Residence Two
Ladera Ranch, California
2003
Pages 124-127

*Bassenian/Lagoni Architects Team:*
*Designers:* Dave Kosco AIA,
Craig Gambill AIA
*Project Manager:* Ken Niemerski AIA

*Builder:* Standard Pacific Homes
*Builder Executives in Charge of Design:*
Todd Palmaer, Ralph Spargo
*Landscape Architect:* Summers/Murphy
& Partners
*Interior Designer:* Design Tec Interiors
*Structural Engineer:* Structural Design
Group

*Photographer:* Lance Gordon

*Awards:*
Best in American Living Awards 2003
Best Community – Platinum Award
Residence 2 – Gold Award
National Sales & Marketing Awards 2003
Residence 2 – Silver & Regional Awards
Gold Nuggets 2003
Site Plan – Grand Award
Residence 2 – Grand Award
MAME Awards/Southern California 2003
Winner

*Magazine Cover:* Builder Magazine,
September 2003

**The Lakes**
The Community
Rancho Santa Fe, California
2007
Pages 84-89

*Bassenian/Lagoni Architects Team*
*Claybourne Product*
  *Designers:* Kevin Karami, Joe Abrajano
  *Project Managers:* Jeff Ganyo,
    Brian Neves AIA, Sophia Braverman,
    Derek Sabor
*Edgewater Product*
  *Designers:* Craig Gambill AIA,
    Raffi Agaian, Ryan Sullivan
  *Project Manager:* Marty Lopez

*Builder:* Lennar
*Builder Executives in Charge of Design:*
  Mike Levesque, Tom Martin
*Landscape Architect:* Pinnacle Design
*Interior Designer:* Pacific Dimensions
*Structural Engineer:* Swanson &
  Associates

*Photographer:* Eric Figge

**MiraBay**
Tradewind Residence
Apollo Beach, Florida
2005
Pages 128-131

*Bassenian/Lagoni Architects Team:*
*Designers:* Hans Anderle, Jason Yaw
*Project Manager:* Mike Beam

*Builder:* Sabal Homes of Florida
*Builder Executive in Charge of Design:*
  Bill Lee
*Landscape Architect:* Dunlap &
  Associates
*Interior Designer:* Creative Design
  Consultants
*Structural Engineer:* Silcox, Kidwell &
  Associates

*Photographer:* Rob/Harris Productions

*Awards:*
National Sales & Marketing Awards 2005
  Gold & Regional Winner
Aurora Awards 2005
  Best Detached Single Family Home
  Best Kitchen
  Best Interior Detailing
  Best Master Bath
Tampa Bay Parade of Homes 2006
  Grand Award
Tampa Bay Parade of Homes 2007
  Grand Award
MiraBay Newland Communities 2006
  Outstanding Architecture
    Grand Award

*Magazine Cover:* Professional Builder,
May 2005

**Montanez at Covenant Hills**
Residence One
Ladera Ranch, California
2005
Pages 114-117

*Bassenian/Lagoni Architects Team:*
*Designers:* Dave Kosco AIA,
  Kevin Karami, Joe Abrajano,
  Raffi Agaian
*Project Managers:* Jeff Ganyo,
  Sophia Braverman

*Builder:* Centex Homes – Southern
  California Coastal Division
*Builder Executives in Charge of Design:*
  Richard Douglass, Nick Lehnert,
  Rick Wood
*Landscape Architect:* Borthwick Guy
  Bettenhausen
*Interior Designer:* Studio Design Group
*Structural Engineer:* Van Dorpe Chou
  Associates

*Photographer:* Anthony Gomez

*Awards:*
MAME Awards/Southern California 2005
  Best Detached Community – Finalist
  Residence 1 – Winner

**Montanez at Covenant Hills**
Residence Three
Ladera Ranch, California
2005
Pages 118-123

*Bassenian/Lagoni Architects Team:*
*Designers:* Dave Kosco AIA,
  Kevin Karami, Joe Abrajano,
  Raffi Agaian
*Project Managers:* Jeff Ganyo,
  Sophia Braverman

*Builder:* Centex Homes – Southern
  California Coastal Division
*Builder Executives in Charge of Design:*
  Richard Douglass, Nick Lehnert,
  Rick Wood
*Landscape Architect:* Borthwick Guy
  Bettenhausen
*Interior Designer:* Studio Design Group
*Structural Engineer:* Van Dorpe Chou
  Associates

*Photographer:* Anthony Gomez

*Awards:*
Gold Nuggets 2006
  Merit Award
MAME Awards/Southern California 2005
  Best Detached Community – Finalist

**The Province**
Residence Four
Indian Wells, California
2007
Pages 64-67

*Bassenian/Lagoni Architects Team:*
*Designers:* Kevin Karami, Raffi Agaian,
  Alan Nguyen
*Project Manager:* Sophia Braverman

*Builder:* Standard Pacific Homes
*Builder Executives in Charge of Design:*
  Ram Fullen, Gary Carlson
*Landscape Architect:* HRP Studio
*Interior Designer:* Meridian Interiors
*Structural Engineer:* Structures Design
  Group

*Photographer:* Anthony Gomez

*Awards:*
Gold Nuggets 2007
  Grand Award

**The Province**
Residence Five
Indian Wells, California
2007
Pages 68-73

*Bassenian/Lagoni Architects Team:*
*Designers:* Kevin Karami, Raffi Agaian,
  Alan Nguyen
*Project Manager:* Sophia Braverman

*Builder:* Standard Pacific Homes
*Builder Executives in Charge of Design:*
  Ram Fullen, Gary Carlson
*Landscape Architect:* HRP Studio
*Interior Designer:* Meridian Interiors
*Structural Engineer:* Structures Design
  Group

*Photographer:* Anthony Gomez

*Awards:*
Gold Nuggets 2007
  Merit Award

**Rimrock Summit**
The Community
Hidden Meadows, California
2006/2007
Pages 52-55

*Bassenian/Lagoni Architects Team:*
*Designers:* Ray Hart, Stacie Arrigo
*Project Managers:* Jeff Ganyo,
  Mike Beam, Marty Lopez

*Builder:* Mastercraft Homes
*Builder Executives in Charge of Design:*
  Daniel Thompson, Bob Liewer
*Landscape Architect:* Land Concern
*Interior Designer:* Blackbird Interiors
*Structural Engineer:* Gouvis Engineering

*Photographer:* Lance Gordon

*Awards:*
Gold Nuggets 2007
  Detached Community – Merit Award
  Residence 1 – Merit Award

**Shady Canyon Residence**
Irvine, California
2006
Pages 32-43

*Bassenian/Lagoni Architects Team:*
*Designers:* Kevin Karami, Joe Abrajano
*Project Manager:* Jeff Marcotte

*Client:* Jeff Roos
*Landscape Architect:* Katzmaier Newell
  Kehr
*Interior Designers:* Dana Blower Design,
  Christopher Kinne
*Structural Engineer:* Gouvis Engineering

*Photographer:* Eric Figge

**Sutter's Mill**
Ladera Ranch, California
2004
Pages 132-137

*Bassenian/Lagoni Architects Team:*
*Designers:* Dave Kosco AIA,
Steven Dewan AIA, John Bigot AIA
*Project Managers:* Jeff Ganyo,
Ian Sparks

*Builder:* Centex Homes – Southern
California Coastal Division
*Builder Executives in Charge of Design:*
Richard Douglass, Nick Lehnert
*Landscape Architect:* Borthwick Guy
Bettenhausen
*Interior Designer:* Rooms Interiors
*Structural Engineer:* Van Dorpe Chou
Associates

*Photographer:* Eric Figge

*Awards:*
Best in American Living Awards 2004
Best Attached Project – Platinum Award
National Sales & Marketing Awards 2004
Residence 4 – Gold and Regional Awards
Gold Nuggets 2005
Attached Project – Grand Award
Attached Project of the Year –
Merit Award
Gold Nuggets 2004
Best Attached Project – Merit Award
American Institute of Architects/Orange
County 2004
Honor Winner
MAME Awards/Southern California 2004
Attached Project – Finalist

*Magazine Cover:*
Professional Builder, November 2004

**Three-65 at Victoria Gardens**
Rancho Cucamonga, California
2007
Pages 104-105

*Bassenian/Lagoni Architects Team:*
*Designers:* Dave Kosco AIA, Raffi Agaian
*Project Manager:* Scott Bunney

*Builder:* Shea Homes
*Builder Executive in Charge of Design:*
Bob Yoder
*Landscape Architect:* The Collaborative
West
*Interior Designer:* Garrett Interiors
*Structural Engineer:* ESI/FME

*Photographer:* Will Hare, Jr.

*Awards:*
Gold Nuggets 2007
Attached Project – Merit Award
Attached Project of the Year –
Merit Award

**The Tides at Crystal Cove**
Residence One
Newport Coast, California
2007
Pages 14-25

*Bassenian/Lagoni Architects Team:*
*Designers:* Kevin Karami,
Dave Kosco AIA, Joe Abrajano,
*Project Manager:* Brian Neves AIA

*Builder:* Standard Pacific Homes –
Gallery Communities
*Builder Executives in Charge of Design:*
Todd Palmaer, Ralph Spargo
*Landscape Architect:* Summers/Murphy
& Partners
*Interior Designer:* Pacific Dimensions
*Structural Engineer:* Structures Design
Group

*Photographer:* Anthony Gomez

**Tremezzo at Lake Las Vegas**
Residence Two
Henderson, Nevada
2007
Pages 44-47

*Bassenian/Lagoni Architects Team:*
*Designers:* Hans Anderle, Jeff Lake AIA,
Stacie Arrigo, Will Francisco
*Project Manager:* Brian Cameron

*Builder:* Pardee Homes
*Builder Executives in Charge of Design:*
Bob Clauser, Loren Smets
*Landscape Architect:* SJA
*Interior Designer:* Color Design Art
*Structural Engineer:* Borm Associates

*Photographer:* Eric Figge

**Wine Country Residence**
Paso Robles, California
2006
Pages 90-103

*Bassenian/Lagoni Architects Team:*
*Designers:* Steven Dewan AIA,
John Bigot AIA
*Project Manager:* Mike Beam

*Builder:* Woody Woodruff Construction
Company
*Landscape Architect:* Land Concern
*Interior Designer:* Marilyn Riding Design
*Construction Documents:* Randall Barnett
*Structural Engineer:* Jeffrey Schneidereit
Architects
*Lighting Consultant:* Linda Ferry Lighting
Design

*Photographer:* Eric Figge

*Awards:*
Gold Nuggets 2007
Merit Award
MAME Awards/Southern California 2007
Best Custom Home – Winner

**Al Khobar Lakes**
Retail Center
Saudi Arabia
2007
Pages 142-143

*Bassenian/Lagoni Architects Team:*
*Designer:* Ali Badie AIA

*Builder:* Emaar
*Builder Executives in Charge of Design:*
  Mark Amirault, Nasreldain Mahamoud

**Luxury Villas**
East OCT
Shenzhen, China
2007
Pages 148-149

*Bassenian/Lagoni Architects Team:*
*Designer:* Wenfei Feng

*Builder:* Overseas China Town Co., Ltd.
*Builder Executives in Charge of Design:*
  Jian Dian, Judy Qiao

*Graphics:* Archiwood Design
  Development

**Mohali Hills**
Villa Homes
Chandigarh, India
2007
Pages 144-145

*Bassenian/Lagoni Architects Team:*
*Designers:* Albern Yolo, Robert Orosa AIA

*Builder:* Emaar/MGF
*Builder Executive in Charge of Design:*
  Scott Pottruff

*Rendering:* AMP 3D Zone

**Tinja**
Townhomes
Tangier, Morocco
2007
Pages 146-147

*Bassenian/Lagoni Architects Team:*
*Designers:* Ali Badie AIA, Romeo Ty,
  Kevin Karami

*Builder:* Emaar/Morocco
*Builder Executives in Charge of Design:*
  Wafaa Snibla
  Turner International

*Rendering:* AMP 3D Zone

**Umm Al Quwain**
Marina & Golf Resort
United Arab Emirates
2006
Pages 140-141

*Bassenian/Lagoni Architects Team:*
*Designer:* Ali Badie AIA

*Builder:* Emaar
*Builder Executives in Charge of Design:*
  Scott Pottruff, Sana Farooq

*Rendering:* Michael Abbott

**Urban Infill Community**
California
2006
Pages 150-151

*Bassenian/Lagoni Architects Team:*
*Designers:* Ali Badie AIA,
  Paul Fulbright AIA

*Rendering:* Milo Olea

# Staff List 2007

## Executive Staff
Aram Bassenian
Carl Lagoni
Scott Adams
Ali Badie
Steven Dewan
Kevin Karami
Dave Kosco
Jeff LaFetra
Jeff Lake
Ken Niemerski
Lee Rogaliner

## Vice Presidents
Mike Beam
Robert Chavez
Ernie Gorrill
Nick Lehnert
Brian Neves
Dave Pockett

## Vice President, China Operations
Yao Wang

## Director of Marketing
Heather McCune

## Associate Vice Presidents
Hans Anderle
Craig Gambill
Jeff Ganyo
Marty Lopez
Edie Motoyama
Robert Orosa

## Senior Associates
John Bigot
Sophia Braverman
Ray Hart
Jeff Marcotte

## Associates
Kevin Burt
Brian Cameron
Dave Day
Judy Forrester
George Handy
Curtis Ong
Tony Vinh
Wendy Woolsey

## General Staff
Joe Abrajano
Raffi Agaian
Stacie Arrigo
Edwin Balquiedra
Jesse Barrera
Rafael Bello
Karen Bestone
Bruce Bishara
Randy Brown
Scott Bunney
Dwayne Butz
Eva Caranay
Lenz Casilan
Sergio Cecena
Luis Chavez
Johnny Chung
Freddy Conrado
Sue Dewan
Jenni Dillon
Kele Dooley
Dee Drylie
Maleck Elahi
Ginger Elkins
Gerry Encarnacion
Alicia Erickson
Todd Evans
Jorge Favila
Joey Feld
Wenfei Feng
Jornell Franciliso
Will Francisco
Paul Fulbright
Casey Galyean
Mike Gilbert
Kevin Groves
Joohyun Her
Young Hong
Roberta Jeannette
Alison Jones
Joel Jose
Erik Kelenc
James Kim
Alan Knebel
John Kounlavong
Huy Le
Mark Leasor
Jason Lee
Ji Sun Lee
Phillip Lee
David McClean
Kristina McVeigh
Jose Mendez

Carlos Meneses
Laura Minott
Tom Mkhitaryan
Christina Nagel
Alan Nguyen
Ronnie Ojeda
Jacob Olid
John Oravetz
Carlos Pelayo
Margo Penick
Jeremy Phillips
Mike Pilarski
Susan Pistacchi
Rachel Pockett
Gregory Purvis
Tarane Rahmani
Yvonne Ramos
Rod Reyes
Jeff Roach
Nate Rodholm
Ryan Rosecrans
Erin Ryan
Derek Sabor
Katya Sato
Selma Saxton
Jesika Scherzinger
Anna Shakun
Andrew Silder
Jeffry Sinarjo
Debora Smith
Tracy Smith
Ian Sparks
Dawn Stanton
Michael Stone
Kevin Stracner
Ellen Sung
Janet Thomas
Romeo Ty
Chris Velasquez
Linda Velasquez
April Villa
Long Vu
Warren Walker
Jill Warren
James West-Herr
Ryan White
Eric Widmer
John Wilmert
Michael Wu
Wenling Wu
Albern Yolo
Bernard Yuen

# Index

# R

# S

# T

# U

# V

# Y

# Memoirs of
# a Russian Lady

# Memoirs of
# a Russian Lady

Drawings and Tales of Life Before the Revolution

MARIAMNA DAVYDOFF

*Selected and edited by Olga Davydoff Dax*

*Harry N. Abrams, Inc., Publishers, New York*

*Photography by Jean Pierre Pavillard*
*Designed by Sue Ebrahim*

*Library of Congress Cataloging-in-Publication Data*

*Davydoff, Mariamna Adrianovna, 1871–1961.*
  *Memoirs of a Russian lady.*

  *1. Davydoff, Mariamna Adrianovna, 1871–1961.*
*2. Soviet Union—Biography. I. Dax, Olga Davydoff.*
*II. Title.*
*CT1218.D38A36   1986   947.08′092′4 [B]   86–3361*
*ISBN 0-8109-0839-5*

*Copyright © 1986 Thames and Hudson Ltd, London*

*Published in 1986 by Harry N. Abrams, Incorporated, New York*
*All rights reserved. No part of the contents of this book may be*
*reproduced without the written permission of the publishers*

*Times Mirror Books*

*Printed and bound in Hong Kong*

# CONTENTS

# PREFACE

IN THE AUTUMN of 1983 I was travelling in the United States and called on a distant cousin of mine, Elena Lvovna Vassiloff, who lives on Long Island. Like me, she was born Davydoff and descended from Vassily Lvovich Davydoff, who had been exiled to Siberia because of his role in the Decembrist plot of 1825, when young Russian nobles made an unsuccessful attempt to overthrow the Tsar. Vassily Lvovich was her great-grandfather and my great-great-grandfather. Elena Lvovna, or Aliona, as she is called (a phonetic translation, always a problem when rendering Russian into a Western language), told me that she had three albums that her mother, Mariamna Adrianovna Davydoff, had left her. When I saw the quality of these little works of art that Mariamna herself had painted over fifty years earlier and that had remained hidden ever since, I felt they should be published — and that is how the idea of the present book was born.

Mariamna Adrianovna, the author of this book, was born Lopukhin, an old Russian family whose origins can be traced back to the eleventh century and whose ancestor Eudoxia married Peter the Great. The Lopukhins had been extremely wealthy and owned vast estates in the Ukraine; but Mariamna's grandfather, a notorious spendthrift, squandered his share of the family fortune, as did his brother's only son, so that Mariamna's father and his close relatives found themselves almost destitute.

On her mother's side, Mariamna came from an old and illustrious family, several of whose members played important roles in Russian history. Her mother's father, Ivan Orlov, was a Cossack chief and an extremely wealthy landowner; but here again his only son depleted the family fortune and was even forced to sell the family seat, Matussov. Mariamna's parents decided to buy Matussov in order to keep it in the family. To do this they not only had to sell the small estate her mother had received as a dowry, but also had to borrow from the banks. This put them in debt for the rest of their lives, and as the huge house and estate required a large staff and was very expensive to run they were forced to live in strict seclusion.

Mariamna was the second of five daughters, one of whom died in the 1890s. To recover from this sad event the family left Matussov for the first time and travelled to Paris, where Mariamna studied painting at the Académie Julian.

In 1899 Mariamna married Lev Alexeyevich Davydoff, a grandson of the Decembrist Vassily Lvovich, whose wife, Alexandra Ivanovna, was one of eleven heroic women that followed their husbands into exile. This couple had thirteen children, six born before the exile and seven after. Of the six, four were born before Vassily and Alexandra were married; Vassily's mother had opposed the match, and it was only after her death in January 1825 that they were able to marry. They had two sons before Vassily was sent to Siberia: Pyotr Vassilyevich, born in 1825, who married the daughter of another Decembrist, Prince Sergey Petrovich Trubetskoy (they were my great-grandparents), and Nicholas Vassilyevich, born in 1826, who never married. After Vassily Lvovich's condemnation these two became the sole legitimate heirs of the family estates which Vassily had inherited and from which he was deprived along with his rights and privileges.

The most important of these estates was the vast domain of Kamenka, which had been inherited through Prince Grigory Alexandrovich Potemkin, the well-known favourite of Catherine the Great. The nucleus of the estate was situated next to the village of Kamenka about 250 km south of Kiev. It comprised hundreds of thousands of hectares and included three large farming enterprises, Podlesnoe, Pliakovsky and Nikolaevsky, as well as many smaller estates where various members of the family settled and which became independent.

After leaving the army, the bachelor Nicholas Vassilyevich settled down in Kamenka and devoted his life to restoring it to its old status, whereas Pyotr went to live on his wife's estate in the Crimea. Nicholas never left Kamenka. He lived there with two of his unmarried sisters, Elisaveta ("Aunt Lisa"), born in 1823 before her parents' marriage, and Alexandra ("Aunt Sasha"), born in 1831 in Siberia.

One of the sons born in Siberia was Alexis Vassilyevich, the father of Mariamna's husband. Another one, Lev Vassilyevich, took over the management of the Kamenka estate, thus enabling Nicholas to devote his time to the study of philosophical, social and economic subjects. Lev Vassilyevich married Alexandra Ilyinishna, the sister of the composer Pyotr Ilyich Tchaikovsky, and they settled in Verbovka, a few kilometres from the village of Kamenka. Of their seven children, Yuri became the curator of the Tchaikovsky Museum in Klin where he died in 1965 (to be succeeded by his daughter Ksenya), and Dimitry ("Mitya") took over the Verbovka estate.

Another section of the Kamenka domain, known as Yurchikha, was given by Pyotr Vassilyevich to his only son, Vassily, my grandfather, who died in 1900. His widow, born Princess Olga Lieven, lived there with her three sons, the youngest of whom, Alexander Vassilyevich, was my father.

"Uncle Nicholas", who appears so often in Mariamna's paintings, lived in Kamenka in what was known as the Green House. It still exists and has become a museum called the Pushkin and Tchaikovsky Museum because of the frequent and prolonged visits that these two illustrious men made to Kamenka. Aunt Lisa and Aunt Sasha lived in the "big" house where another sister, Vera, who was married and lived in St Petersburg, often stayed.

After 1905 Mariamna and her husband Lev Alexeyevich lived for many years with their daughter Aliona in one of the smaller houses at Kamenka. Lev ran the estate and its sugar refinery, and gradually took over the whole enterprise. As early as 1906 Nicholas Vassilyevich made a will bequeathing the whole estate to him. In 1908 Lev bought another property, Dubrova, situated not far from Kamenka, and from that time on he, Mariamna and Aliona divided their time between Kamenka and Dubrova.

At the outbreak of war in 1914 Lev was mobilized, as were most of the men working on the various farms and estates of Kamenka. Mariamna and Aliona went to live in Kiev and when the bolsheviks overran the city they managed to reach Odessa. From there they went to Constantinople, then to Rome, and finally to Paris, where they lived until 1924 in very straitened circumstances. In 1924 they went to live in Concarneau, Brittany, where Mariamna's elder sister Juliet lived with her French husband and where both her parents were buried. In 1932 Mariamna returned to Paris and in 1949 she emigrated to the United States, where she died in 1961.

Since the original text of Mariamna's memoirs and all the watercolours had been destroyed in Russia before she left, she decided, while living in Concarneau, to reproduce them from memory for her granddaughter Irina, the daughter of Aliona. Her talent as a painter was such that she was able to capture in her watercolours the likeness of all the people she had known in Russia. She was intent on reproducing everything, down to the smallest details such as the design of the wallpaper, the fabric of the dresses or the material covering armchairs and sofas. She felt this was essential to convey what life had really been like in Russia before the Revolution among the families of well-to-do landowners and what the condition of the peasants and the servants had been. She left this wonderful heritage to her daughter, her granddaughter, and her great-grandchildren; and I am grateful to them for having agreed to let others share extracts from Mariamna's story through the publication of this book.

OLGA DAVYDOFF DAX

# 1 Matussov

OUR HOUSE, a country estate called Matussov in the province of Kiev in southern Russia, was a splendid building, virtually a château and much too vast for our means. It required twelve servants to run it: six women and six men. The women slept in a large room next to my parents' bedroom and each had a small iron bed. The men slept downstairs as best they could, some behind a small curtain in the pantry and the younger ones on the floor.

During the day, the maintenance man, Zossim, often sat in a recess under the staircase (where he also slept), an enormous Book of Psalms open on his knees, reading and humming for hours; nobody ever interfered or reproached him for not working. Zossim was very pious.

My father's manservant, Matvei, was a small ageless man, always neatly turned out and ready to serve. He adored Papa and looked after him like a child, and when, after my father's death, my mother sold the estate and Matvei went back to his home in the village, he couldn't restrain himself from returning to the empty, abandoned château and cleaning father's room as he had always done, dusting and looking after the furniture as if my father were still alive.

In my childhood a chaplain officiated in the chapel that was part of the house, but as a result of the intrigues of a priest from another parish, the ecclesiastical authorities asked my parents to get rid of him. From then on very few services were celebrated in our chapel – only at Christmas, at Easter, and on the birthday of a member of the family.

In spite of this, Zossim would continue to put on the night-lights by the icons every Saturday evening, and when we walked by the chapel we would be frightened to see through the cloudy, wire-meshed windows those feeble lights that seemed to us like manifestations of the Great Beyond.

Zossim, our pious manservant, reading his Psalms in a niche under the
stairs and looking after the lamps

*Our private chapel at Matussov:*

*the family on one side, the servants on the other*

As in every Russian country home, our bakery had a special importance. Baba Odarka, the bakerwoman, reigned supreme there. She baked fresh bread every day, but undertook a great many other tasks, particularly on holidays. She made delicate doughs that rose and fell at the slightest noise. The air was filled with the aromas of vanilla, cinnamon and lemon zest. A splendid plum cake stood next to brioches covered with sugar and almonds, and there were many other delicious things in preparation as Odarka kneaded a soft and pleasant swelling dough on the table.

The main courtyard of the house was followed by a succession of equally spacious courtyards, and off these were the outbuildings, the stables, the pigsty, the dairy, the store rooms, the cellars, etc. There were four separate wings, each consisting of six to eight rooms. The kitchen and the bakery were in one of these wings, in addition to a separate staff kitchen, and a sort of Turkish *hammam*. In my grandfather's day, the rooms in the other three wings were all for guests. He loved to entertain and would occasionally give sumptuous parties that lasted several days.

In my time, only one guest-room wing remained, and it was hardly ever used for that purpose because my parents almost never entertained. There was no superfluous luxury in our home, if one discounts the numerous domestics, the silverware on the immaculate tablecloth, and the four servants who waited at table. A strict etiquette prevailed: the children were not allowed to speak at table, and if one of us happened to bend forward Papa would strike the table with his hand, a reminder for us to keep our backs straight.

Other estates indulged in an overwhelming luxury; even in mid-winter, silver and vermeil vases were filled with lily-of-the-valley and roses. But Mama, who had always lived in the country, had her own ideas on these matters. Furthermore, she had been a young girl when the great reforms took place in Russia, and the emancipation of the serfs was proclaimed. Families like hers reduced their style of living; many even locked themselves in their houses and refused to entertain any more. Because of this, Mama grew up in straitened circumstances. When she married my father, Adrian Adrianovich Lopukhin, who was himself not well off, her dowry included a lovely estate near Matussov, where they settled down and lived as recluses.

When my mother's father died, his only son inherited the Matussov estate. He was a *bon vivant* who paid no attention to business and regarded his inheritance as nothing more than a means of acquiring ready money. The inevitable result was that he was forced to sell the property. My parents, who lived 15 km away, were the buyers.

*Notre boulangère particulière.*

Our bakery at Matussov, in the charge of Baba Odarka

*La chambre des femmes de chambres*

*Our housemaids dealing with the linen on a wintry afternoon*

ONE OF MAMA'S older sisters lived on an estate 50 km from Matussov, and this was one of the rare homes that we would visit. We used to be taken there, with the maids and governesses, once or twice a year in an omnibus that Papa had bought at Bellevolette's in Paris. Conrad, our confectioner, or Papa's valet Matvei sat next to the coachman. The trunks, and sometimes a young manservant or a chambermaid, sat on the upper deck. Mama, Papa, relatives or friends followed in victorias or coupés. The omnibus, drawn by six horses, advanced slowly because the tracks were often a sea of mud, and each time one of the travellers asked for something to eat or drink, or whatever, the whole caravan would come to a halt. At the halfway point there was a Jewish coaching inn where fresh horses, sent ahead the day before, were awaiting us. The servants brought out the hampers and then we would eat for two whole hours. One day we asked the innkeeper for borscht, the national soup of the Ukraine, and he brought us a chamberpot full of the delicious soup!

18

Our aunt's estate was like an oasis in the middle of the steppe. It was a lovely large house of red brick, surrounded by a huge park. In summer we would stop at the very end of the park and, while the coaches with the servants drove around it through the village, we would walk down the alley that led straight to the house.

The house had a huge lawn in front of it that sloped gently down to a pond, behind which the steppe extended into infinity. There were spacious rooms – a blue salon and a pink salon, a billiard room, an enormous dining room where, after each meal, a dwarf burnt perfume on a red-hot shovel. Aunt and Uncle had five daughters and one son who were our age, and there were masses of servants, maids and governesses, just as there were at Matussov.

*Driving in the spring mud on a visit to our aunt's estate*

*Conrad, our confectioner, performing one of his sweet miracles*

A HUNDRED YEAR OLD mulberry tree with many trunks used to grow in front of the dining room windows. It was thick and stocky, with massive branches, one of which hung horizontally over the wide lane that bordered the house, and we loved to climb up it in summer.

Conrad, our confectioner, who had been a serf in his youth but was a white-haired old man by the time I knew him, would cook his jams most of the time under the mulberry tree.

Conrad was a real magician in his profession. He had been sent by my Orlov grandfather to train with the best confectioner in St. Petersburg. He came back a true expert in this art and his whole life long he stuffed my family with delicious pastries and sweets. In normal times he did the same chores as the other servants; only on great occasions, such as birthdays or holidays, would he disappear mysteriously into the kitchen to create his marvels. We would go secretly to watch him at work, licking our lips in anticipation at the

Maman et le confiseur Conrad s'appliquent aux confitures

Conrad cooking jam under our old mulberry tree

Гаданіе.

The season called "gadanie",
when we picked branches from our cherry trees

sight of an almond-paste pyramid on the various levels of which appeared many diverse mushroom-shaped biscuits made of chocolate, sugared hazel nuts, caramelized nuts, *langues de chat*, patience dock leaves with aniseed . . . He also made all the jams, the crystallized fruit, and many other delicacies. He had a superb voice, a deep bass, and sang in the choir when there were services in the chapel.

O N 24 NOVEMBER, St. Catherine's day, we would rise before dawn, go out in the garden and pick branches of cherry trees, put them into a bottle filled with water, and make a wish, hoping that they would blossom before the 1st of January. If they did, the wish would be granted. . . . In fact, they blossomed only rarely; I have seen it happen only once or twice in my lifetime.

The days between 24 November and 6 January were known as "gadanie", which meant the time when one consulted the fates and drew lots by means of all sorts of witchcraft to guess the future and especially anything that had to do with love and marriage.

T HE MOST THRILLING PROCEDURE was the seance in the *hammam*. We never really had the courage to do it. One had to sit there with two lit candles between the two facing mirrors. They and the lights reflected from one to the other created a long corridor, at the end of which was supposed to appear the most significant event of the year. The apparition did not arrive right away. Often one had to wait for hours alone at night. Our chambermaids told us that some young girls had seen coffins and that they had died during the year; others had seen wedding processions and had married!

The *hammam* had been installed in time immemorial and though it was replaced by bathrooms it still had its advantages. On Saturdays the chambermaids came to fetch us and led us to the *hammam*. Outdoors was a wintry night. We crossed the courtyard, the snow crackling under our feet, the sky unfathomable and the stars shining and vibrating in the frozen air. When the door of the *hammam* was opened, clouds of steam poured out. One of the chambermaids sprayed the huge boiler with water, another prepared the basins for washing our hair, a third heated the towels.

The same winter picture awaited us on our way back to the main house: the hard menacing sky and the snow singing under our "valenkis" – felt-lined boots.

*Hamam tout les Samedis.*

*The* hammam *at Matussov*

FOR AT LEAST the first ten years after Papa got into debt in order to buy Matussov, we suffered from a severe lack of money. This meant that we had nothing which had to be bought, such as new clothes or presents, and obviously no Christmas tree. There was a young mechanic working in our sugar factory, a Czech who, when he heard that we would have no Christmas tree, made one for us in the form of a pivoting tower that was rotated by the heat of the candles.

On Christmas Eve at about 5, the main salon was closed and we were forbidden to enter. It wasn't until much later, when we saw the rising of the first star in the icy cold sky, that we were invited to step into the salon. We stood on the threshold, filled with wonder and blinded by what was in the room. At first the candles on the mechanical tree prevented us from seeing anything but their flickering lights. Then, however, we began gradually to distinguish, on the platforms tapering upwards, animals, little men, birds, all in sugar or caramel. The mechanic who had created this looked at us with a gratified smile, pleased by the effect his work of art had had on us.

*Un arbre de Noël mécanique et tournant.*

*The mechanical Christmas tree*

AFTER THEIR MARRIAGE, neither of my parents ever really had fun out of life. As I and my sisters appeared, they became increasingly occupied with their large and time-consuming household. Nor did they ask anything more of life. Neither their isolated existence at Matussov nor the long winter months disturbed them. Mama could spend hours on end winding balls out of lamb's wool that had been spun by women in the village, and Papa would be downstairs in his study sculpting works of art in wood, making frames, boxes, etc. On the threshold of his study we would often see a Jew dressed in the traditional long frockcoat and with curls over his ears, negotiating for the wheat of the coming year, or testing the ground for the sale of old oxen or farm houses. "Well, Adrian Adrianovich," he would ask shyly, "how much wheat have you sown this year?"

Papa would blow away the shavings and sawdust from the wood, then mutter between two breaths, "Five hundred hectares." "Yes, I knew that already," said the Jew whose name was Yutka; "how much are you selling it for?" "Eighty kopecks," answered Papa. "I was told it was 79 kopecks," said Yutka, and Papa flew into a rage. But Yutka had already disappeared . . . which did not prevent him from returning the following day and many days after that, at the very same spot and asking exactly the same questions.

My parents had a number of pet occupations. Our courtyard was filled with carpenters, sculptors, blacksmiths who made all sorts of artistic objects under Papa's watchful eye – the "staircase of honour" with its carved banisters, wrought-iron lamp posts, and cupboards carved with designs taken from coloured albums Papa had brought back from Paris. Mama preferred living objects, animals of all sorts, and unfortunately she would get so absorbed by them that she tended to neglect me and my sisters in both our emotional and our psychological development.

We were very pious and as long as our priest, Father Nicholas, who was paid by us, conducted his services in our chapel we attended regularly. Mama, who loved music and had a good voice, had organized a choir, in which the principal singers were Conrad (bass), Zossim (an insignificant tenor), and another servant, Effim (a superb tenor). Mama was the soprano and a number of local boys completed the choir. The rehearsals took place in the large circular salon and were a real treat for us. We listened as in a trance but were not allowed to take part.

*Le studio de mon père Adrien Lopoukhine.*

Papa in his study

THE CHURCH of the Ascension was 3 km from Matussov. Its priest, Father Agathon, was said to be the offspring of one of grandfather Orlov's escapades with a gypsy woman. Whether this was true or not, we loved him very much.

It was not often that we were taken to church, especially in winter when it was feared that we might catch cold. But since it was compulsory at the great holy days, we stood in church on the clear and cold morning of December 25th. There was a lot of snow that winter and the church windows were all frosty and blue. We sat in our usual pews on the left and looked at the other people, the young peasant girls with their heads covered in flowers and ribbons, the police representative straight and solemn in his ceremonial suit, and some unknown people in the choir on the right. They looked like strangers, for their clothes were different from those we were used to seeing. After a moment's thought we came to the conclusion that they must be Father Agathon's children.

The service comes to an end. People start leaving and Mama wishes to speak to Father Agathon. She moves close to the altar and we wait there among freezing gusts for him to appear. Ah! Here he is at last, with a smile on his lips. Mama asks him to come the following evening to say vespers at our home at 6 and mass the day after that in our chapel. Out of the corner of our eyes we see the strangers stepping down from the choir. "Here are my children," stutters Father Agathon, "step forward, step forward . . . th . . . th . . . they have come for the feast fr . . . fr . . . from Kiev. Sasha, Yulya . . . There you are!"

We and the children gawk at each other. Mama says, "So that's decided for tomorrow evening!"

We leave the church and climb into our sleighs. We are all wrapped up in furs. It is a glorious day, sparkling with frost, about 10 degrees below zero.

Tired of waiting, the horses gallop off on the snowpath. We look back to see "the children" again, walking in Indian file behind their father along the wooden palisade that borders the presbytery garden.

*Father Agathon conducting Christmas mass in the Church of the Ascension*

THE NEXT EVENING Father Agathon duly arrives at our chapel in a horse-drawn sleigh. The small bell starts ringing under the watchful hand of Zossim to announce the start of the service.

Our seats are on the left, facing the altar. On the right are the choirboys who have been joined by Conrad, Effim, Zossim and Mama. They bend over a yellow-leaved book and by the light of a wax candle decipher Slavonic letters as they sing psalms.

When the service comes to an end the good Father goes up to Mama, and she asks him to bring some of his children to mass tomorrow. And so the next morning we gather again for mass. Father Agathon appears through the central door, holding a gold cup in his hands. This is the moment for communion. "This is the flesh and the blood of Our Lord Jesus Christ," he proclaims.

After mass, the priests and the choirboys hasten to the out-buildings where a meal awaits them. The deacon is taken by Conrad and Zossim to the pantry where he is offered coffee. Father Agathon and his sons are invited to the house where coffee is served, with biscuits and cakes on a beautiful silver tray.

The young men say Thank you and we take them to another room to get better acquainted. They are so nice in their navy blue uniforms with silver buttons. Palya especially is a very handsome boy; he must be about 14. They are thoughtful and sociable; they talk, tell stories, and even sing "Drink some Tokay wine and your heart will be merry." They are the first young men we have ever met, and we are all aflutter at the sight of Palya's sky-blue eyes. He tells us that they are five girls and five boys.

In the main salon Father Agathon is preparing to leave and calls his sons. "So it's agreed," he says to Mama. "At the New Year m..m..my children will be expecting . . ."

They have hardly left when we pounce on Mama. "What is happening for the New Year? Are you taking us to church? What will the children be expecting? Please tell us, Mama!" And she finally says that we are invited to spend the afternoon at the presbytery. We go mad with joy at this news, we shout and dance. At last we are going to meet them all!

It was bitterly cold at the New Year. The whole of nature seemed petrified by frost. The smoke rose from the cottages straight and blue, as if motionless in the light grey velvety and opaque sky, as in a Japanese drawing. Covered in bear and wolf furs we drove in a sleigh to Father Agathon's presbytery.

It resembled a cottage but was much larger. As we approached it seemed to be sunk in the snow, its windows only 75 cm above the ground. Generally speaking, the priests in the Ukraine were very well off because the peasants in their parishes were prosperous. Thus

La fête de Maman.

*Father Agathon having coffee in our house*

*Christmas carols outside Father Agathon's snow-covered presbytery*

Father Agathon owned cows, pigs, good horses, coaches, servants, and even a 500-hectare estate, 20 km from Matussov, with a nice house and outbuildings.

We were not the only guests that New Year's Day. There were other priests, some with their families, others with only their wives, who sat in a row under the icons, drinking one glass of tea after another. We young ones were piled up in the girls' room where narrow iron beds were lined up against the walls. Father Agathon's children were entertaining us: Palya sang, Petya played the fool, pretty Sasha with the curly golden hair laughed with my sister Juliet while I philosophized with Yulya. "Everyone in the dance room," rang out a voice in the doorway and Masha appeared striking her hands. "We are going to dance," she said laughingly and pushed us out of the overheated room one after another. She was a student at the Moscow Conservatory and already played the piano beautifully. Masha played a furious waltz while couples took to the floor that had been waxed to make it more slippery. Every minute servants passed around trays of candies, chocolates, caramels, nuts, figs, dates, pistachios, hazel nuts, gingerbread, crystallized fruits . . . We had never been to such a party!

*Mama visiting in Father Agathon's house*

Bal chez le prêtre le père Agathon.

*A dance at Father Agathon's*

WE HAD NICKNAMED HIM Chikotini, an italianized name for a consumptive. He was a schoolteacher and also head of the choir in Father Agathon's church. He was a very good musician, and naturally I became his sentimental victim. My love lasted several years; the charm of Panthelemon (his real name) was that he corresponded exactly to the type of sweetheart I dreamed of. He was young, tall, thin and fair (at least that was how I saw him), and above all he was consumptive! He was nervous and jumpy, and each time he started coughing he raised his hands to his head or his chest, which always caused me great emotion. I was filled with joy when, after giving the pitch, he extended his hands and gave the choir the signal to begin a psalm or a prayer, his foot beating time.

This crush of mine was touching and at the same time comical. It was closely linked to our visits to church and to Father Agathon's family. When we went horseback riding we would always try to pass next to the presbytery and would cast tender looks at the cottage next door, which was the school where Chikotini lived. When services took place in our chapel, Chikotini would come over the day before with his choirboys to rehearse with Mama. We listen enthralled to the religious songs led by *his* expert hands. I only had eyes for *him* in his rather overlong frockcoat, totally immersed in his art.

We never spoke to each other, not ever, but what did that matter?

*Répetition avec la maitrise.*     *Tchikotini.*

*My first crush, the schoolteacher Chikotini, with the choirboys*

I N   O U R   C H I L D H O O D, governesses came and went with noticeable speed. Entire
months would elapse without Mama being able to find one willing to come and work in
our "hole". Up to the end of our schooling we had twenty-five of them in all.

One was named Natulia Bernadsky. She was a splendid girl of 16 whose father, a doctor,
had begged Mama to take her, "to hide her", he said, because she was so beautiful. She was
supposed to give us lessons but at 9 we would still be waiting for her; she liked to stay in bed
until 10.

In the autumn, Mama's brother, Uncle David Orlov, arrived for the hunting season. He
was a jolly little man with fiery eyes in a handsome face, a spendthrift and a philanderer. He
was an officer of His Majesty the Emperor's Cossacks, and he was struck by Natulia's beauty.
One morning when the men prepared to leave for the hunt, they were just settling into the
coaches in front of the porch and the servants were bringing the hampers, when Natulia
rushed out on the balcony overlooking the porch and poured a jar of water onto Uncle
David's head. In a rage he rushed up the stairs, seized Natulia in his arms and boorishly
kissed her a dozen times, then ran back down as fast as he could, leaving the young girl
entirely confused, scarlet and upset to the verge of tears. In spite of this, she continued to
tease him. One day he put a cigarette out in her ear. Shortly afterwards Mama asked her
father to take her back.

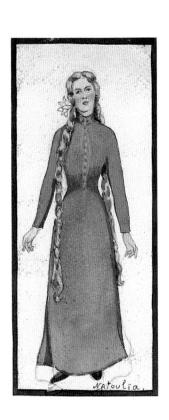

Natoulia.

Ida was small and round with an alarming face. As soon as our homework and lessons
were over, she would be off to the village and stay there for hours. She was silent and
mysterious, but Mama learnt that during her daily absences she would visit peasants and
preach Marxism, which we called nihilism, to them. She did not last long after that.

Lady Charlotte was disfigured, a hunchback as the result of a case of tuberculosis (or
perhaps scarlet fever) when she was 7. When still an adolescent, she left her large family in
England and travelled in many countries, ending up in Russia with the idea of teaching
English to children. She worked first for my mother's sister, Princess Sophia Kudachev, and
then came to us. She taught us French and English, and was gentle, gay and subtle, unlike
Mama or the other governesses who lost patience and punished us. She always wore black
satin dresses with a long train, a bonnet made of black lace that fell down over her poor
hump, and a chinpiece.

Lady Charlotte distribue des récompences pour des reponses bien faites aux leçons.

*Three of our many governesses: Natulia, Ida and Lady Charlotte*

Ida la gouvernante nihiliste.

AT EPIPHANY, on January 6th, we were invited to the presbytery for an afternoon and evening dance. After mass everyone, the priest and the choir in the lead, banners in front, went to the pond to bless the water. The priest said prayers at the foot of a big cross hewn out of the ice, then plunged a silver cross into the pond and gave the blessing.

Since our first meeting with Father Agathon's children we had become better acquainted and we felt totally at ease with them. I never stopped dancing with his son Petya, who claimed to be in love with me.

We stayed for dinner, which was served on long narrow tables. The meal was varied and copious, and lots of vodka was drunk. The borscht was fatty and rich. The priests, bent very low over the table, lapped it up with relish. It ran down their beards and their moustaches dipped into it. After the zakusky and the borscht we were served with many sorts of fish with salted cucumbers, marinated fruits and apple preserved in a special brine: then came the turn of the roast, chicken, turkey, goose with apples, followed by a dessert and oranges, tea with cakes and pastries. Two full hours were spent at the table, and the ball lasted until midnight.

IT IS THE BEGINNING of Lent. The snow is grey and so are the days. We wander in the park, caught up in a wave of poetic melancholy, searching with our feet for last year's blackened leaves.

The seven weeks of Lent always marked our lives. The first week everyone fasted. We were allowed no meat, no eggs, no butter and for some people even no sugar. For us Lent symbolized the awakening of nature, the tender spring that followed the long cold months of bad weather and a closed-in existence in overheated and unventilated rooms.

During Holy Week we would perform our Easter duties at Father Agathon's, and we waited impatiently for that moment to come. In the meantime we roamed dreamily in the park looking for the first violet. At 4, the bells started ringing in all the churches, calling the faithful to Confession. There they were, trudging along in the mud, lifting their booted feet with difficulty out of the sticky compost.

Holy Thursday was the opening day of the series of great religious services that marked Passion Week. We spent the whole day waiting for the evening service when Father Agathon, in a solemn atmosphere, would read twelve passages from the Gospels on the Passion of Jesus Christ.

We gulped our food down as soon as we heard the sound of the coach outside. Then we piled into the "lineika", a wide carriage with several seats. The horses advanced at a walking pace, slipping as they sank into the black mud.

The church was packed. It was the custom to burn candles during the reading of the Gospels; each person had his own and they lit up the whole church. Here was Father Agathon coming from the altar to read and the divine words vibrated in the overheated atmosphere, blurred in the clouds of incense and faded away in the thick shadows of the high cupola.

*Nous allons aux douzes Évangils le Jeudi Saint*

*Going to the Church in the evening on Holy Thursday*

Between midnight mass on Easter eve and the early morning service, the faithful went home to fetch their Easter fare – the dyed eggs, the roasted suckling pig, the sausages, the cream cheese, the cakes, etc. – which they placed around the church so that the priest could bless it all after the service. This was the age-old custom.

We remained waiting in the church because the priest was coming to our home to bless the already laden table. We waited about one and a half hours, chatting softly in the church that had become dark and silent.

At last the service began again. We were tired. The big windows became bluish and the service ended. We went out, banners leading the way. "Christ is risen! Christ is risen!" burst out everywhere. The peasants appeared in a violet pink glow around the church and were immediately blessed by Father Agathon. He was dressed in silver and gold lamé, and enveloped in the blue smoke from his censer.

We returned home in the cold morning air to find a fragrant coffee awaiting us in the dining room. We ate cakes as daylight gazed at us through the windows on this glorious day of Resurrection. Then we went to bed and slept until one.

Easter Sunday was beautiful, mild and sunny. We spent it loafing around the park or around the Easter table. Finally Nicholas Nicholaevich, the son of our current governess, suggested he read us a short tale he had written. He took us out into the park, and sat Juliet and me on a bench while he sat on the ground amid the flowers and read to us. He put so much feeling into his reading that we were filled with enthusiasm. I was even more moved than Juliet because from the start of his Easter visit Nicholas had singled me out from the rest of my sisters. His little black eyes were always searching for me, observing me. I couldn't guess the meaning of all this, but his continual little game was far from displeasing me, since I did not dislike him at all.

On the day when Nicholas was leaving he came up to me, took me by the arm, and said, "Come with me." I felt my arm gripped tightly, and all of a sudden he bent down and pressed his lips passionately on my hand!

I thought for weeks afterwards that I was in love with him. But since I knew it could never lead to a "proper" marriage, I gradually drove him out of my mind and developed other crushes.

*The outdoor blessing service after midnight mass*

THE WINTER OF 189- ended with a great sadness. In early January, my sister Varinka fell ill. It was diagnosed as typhoid, and in March she died. This calamity had a disastrous effect on Mama. Throughout the year, Mama's grief seemed to get worse daily. She gave up all her occupations and lay in bed for hours suffering from severe migraine, or else she remained distant and indifferent to everything. We had to convince Papa that she urgently needed to be amused, to divert her mind from her grief and to let her develop new ideas. Towards the autumn our plans ripened and we finally decided to spend the winter in no less a place than Paris.

Slowly Mama began to wake up out of her lethargy and to come back to life. That was in November. We needed clothes for the journey, so Mama left one evening for Kiev. On the day of her return, announced as usual by a telegram, we were all agog even at 8 in the morning though we knew perfectly well that she could not possibly arrive until 11. We rushed upstairs with a telescope to scan the road. At last the coach appeared, all muddy with steaming horses!

What wonderful things Mama had bought! Unfortunately everything was either black or dark grey, but it didn't matter, it was for Paris! In no time at all the materials she had chosen were transformed into dresses, blouses, coats, by a Jewish tailor from a nearby village.

The journey was quite comical. Mama, who had not left the country for thirty years except for short visits to Kiev, remembered foreign trains as being unheated, so she dressed us up as if we were going to the North Pole with red flannel pants, gaiters, fur-lined galoshes and warm petticoats. Once on the overheated train, we started peeling off the various layers one by one.

Mama had also said that the trains travelled so fast that there was no time to buy anything in the stations so she brought along a large hamper filled with food. To our surprise, we discovered that, as we were in first class international trains, we had access to a magnificent dining car that followed us all the way to Paris. But we had to eat our own food from the hamper!

*Nous partons pour Paris!!!*

*Our departure for Paris*

For our third winter in Kiev, Mama rented a superb apartment, with a large dancing room and dining room. We gave several parties there, but we were short of young men, so a friend suggested that we invite Lev Davydoff, a young cavalry officer who was on leave following an accident in which he had almost been killed. Tall, handsome, fairhaired and a very good dancer, he came to our parties, but we snubbed him a little because we felt sorry for our own young men who looked so insignificant compared to him.

When we returned to the country we got to know Lev's sister, Tassya, who was a charming young girl, the opposite of her brother, with very dark hair and a dark complexion, shrewd but always ready to laugh, and kind. Naturally Lev was also there and he used to come and see us often.


In the spring and summer of 1899, Lev Davydoff and I saw each other again. He and his sister were constantly organizing picnics, either in Trostianka, a small wood near Kamenka, or in the Big Wood.

One day we went to have tea at Trostianka, and Lev, lying flat on his stomach at my feet, told me so many stupid things that I disliked him intensely. When he suggested that he come with me in my carriage I refused. Tassya laughed at this and I became annoyed, but in spite of the fact that Lev had a confused and disappointed mien I refused to go with him.

As the days passed, however, I thought more and more of him, and missed his company when he was absent.

In September the hunting season began. I went to one of these hunts on a beautiful, calm and golden day. The fallen leaves that formed a Persian carpet under one's feet smelt of musk.

At lunch I sat next to my cousin Marguerite, who must have noticed that I was sad because Lev was not there. She said to me, "Why don't you marry your Levuchka, he is so sweet!" I jumped and mumbled rather bitterly, "But does he like me?" "I think so," she answered.

Two days later I went to see Tassya in the big house. We were sitting together in one of the small rooms when the door suddenly burst open and Lev appeared in full uniform, looking very thin and handsome. I asked why he had lost so much weight and he answered, "Because I have been thinking of you!" Tassya wanted to leave, but he held her back.

The day passed without my realizing it. In the early evening, after a walk and dinner, I went out of doors and sat on a bench. Lev followed and sat next to me. Taking my hand, he

*The winter season is here*

*The modest home of Lev's mother in Kiev*

said in a voice choked with emotion, "I must say something to you." "Say what?" I asked him teasingly. "No, not here," he said, looking towards the house. "Let's go for a walk."

We rose and walked in silence through the courtyard and down a staircase hung over with motionless, yellowing leaves mixed with bright red Virginia creeper. The leaves smelled of amber, that special aroma of a damp September night.

At the crossing of the first alley, Lev took my hand. "This is what I wanted to say to you. I love you and if you agree we will never leave each other . . ."

We stopped in the small narrow lane. My heart was beating in my throat and I whispered, "I agree, but we must speak about it to Mama."

He embraced me. I turned my head and he kissed my forehead. We went quickly back to the house where all the windows and doors on the garden side were open.

48

*A picnic in the woods; Lev lies at my feet*

THE WEDDING was fixed for the 12th of November. Mama and I went to Kiev to order my trousseau, which was very modest because we had little money. Two dozen slips, two nightdresses, two dozen underdrawers, two dozen black silk stockings, two dozen lisle ones, three or four dresses, one pelisse, one otterskin *chapka* with a blue ribbon, two dozen sheets and six pillowcases, table cloths, flower baskets and many sprays of lilac. We called on Lev's mother, Maria Nikolaevna, and left the trousseau there, because Lev and I would have to go through Kiev on our way to Petersburg after the wedding.

Invitations were sent out, and we spent the remaining weeks working out all the details. Two or three days before the wedding, we started to prepare the food, to carve the veal and the lamb. Conrad was busy making various sorts of biscuits, tarts and elaborate sweets.

On the evening of November 11th, Father Agathon said vespers in our church while Lev and I and a friend sat in the big hall and played Makao. It was only at the end of the service that we abandoned our card game and went to church to see what was going on, because after all the service was for us! The servants and villagers lined the walls, and at the far end the iconostasis shone by the light of the candles and the red lanterns. Our old retainer Zossim read in a thin voice the first verse of a hymn.

November 12th is a grey day, gloomy and rainy. The house is packed with people. I come downstairs for lunch but don't feel like talking to anyone. The sooner the ceremony is over, the sooner Lev and I will be alone. My friends dress me to be ready at 3 o'clock. One of them sets the veil and the flowers. I have a wonderful damask printed dress with a long train.

I walk down the big staircase to the hall where all my friends are waiting. I enter the church on Papa's arm. Lev in his white cavalry jacket is waiting, anxious and handsome. The church is full. I am the first to set foot on the satin of the lectern. Everything goes well after all – that is to say, the way things should go for a wedding!

After dinner, at 9, we go to the Tsvetkov station, 8 versts away. Finally we are alone in our own railway coach. Only the conductor comes to ask us if we need anything. I put on my lovely new blue dressing gown and undo my hair. At last alone.

38                                    1899   Mam Leslie  Kasotchka

1899

*Our first apartment: Tsarskoye Selo*

L EV AND I TRAVELLED from Kiev to Petersburg, where we had to wait half an hour for the train to Tsarskoye Selo, where we would be living. We had taken a maid, Masha, with us, a spinster who cried all day long. Lev's coachman was waiting for us at the station and took care of the luggage while we climbed onto a one-horse sleigh and started off for home. It was snowing hard and the "sleigh lane" was already open.

Our apartment looked delightful. A table covered in cream cretonne with large artificial carnations stood in the middle of the drawing room on a red woollen carpet. On the lovely desk near the table was a small vase of scented artificial flowers. One of the doors of the drawing room gave on to Lev's office, the other on to a cloakroom that led to the dining room.

The feeling of being my own mistress was quite new to me, and I never forgot it for the rest of my life. The smooth sheets, the down pillows covered in yellow atlas piqué pillowcases with flounces, the blankets . . . oh, how wonderful it all was! And a husband! This was for me a brand new country, so different from our own Little Russia – other people, Lev's regiment, his interests, his life . . . It was so great a change for me that it made my head spin. I felt drunk and my life seemed to be a fairy tale.

O FTEN TWO of Lev's friends, Gor and Chal, would arrive in town. I believe they worked in some ministry or other. We liked them both very much, and I particularly liked Gor, who was very handsome and elegant. He tried to court me, but I was not ready for that!

After lunch Lev ordered that his horse Vikhr be harnessed in such a way that Gor could slip the reins around his waist, install himself on skis, and ride in this fashion around the parks of Pavlovsk and Tsarskoye Selo.

W HEN WE RETURNED from Matussov we brought back an adorable foal which we named Julik – meaning "rogue" – and we bought from Mitya two very young mares – Veda and Vakhanka – so that when we arrived in Tsarskoye Selo we owned a team of three horses. Lev then bought a large sleigh with bells. How wonderful this all was! Though they were not big, the horses were as fast as arrows. It was very difficult to stop them when they raced down avenues and lanes, and we had to keep our eyes open. One even had great difficulty in simply directing them. They never slowed down in curves and Lev would

*Gor riding around the park, harnessed to our horse Vikhr*

almost fall out of the sleigh as he endeavoured to counterbalance its weight to prevent it from overturning. Calm and phlegmatic, Miron simply held the reins!

We had a lot of incidents with these horses. One day Miron was hitching them up and let go of them for barely a second to take his gloves. They promptly sprang away in the courtyard and galloped out into the street where they raced along between the lamp-posts. They finally struck one of the lamp-posts, which broke Julik's harness, and she rolled like a ball on the sidewalk. The two other horses were unable to negotiate the next curve and came to a halt in front of the house that stood on the corner where Lev, Miron and I, who had run after them, found them and brought them home with no further trouble – but with a broken bridle and a torn harness.

# 2 KAMENKA

52                                                    1904.    M

*Our troika at Tsarskoye Selo*

In 1902 Aliona was born, and two days later Lev was given command of the Fourth Squadron, the very one he had served in. He had to learn his new job and deal with the officers on a different footing. During that winter we had been told that Papa's business affairs were going badly but he never spoke of it when he came to visit. Finally Mama informed us that she could no longer send us any money, things were so bad.

I had already been hinting, and indeed saying aloud, that Lev should leave his regiment and devote his strength and energy to better things. He would always reply that one had to have something else in view before taking such a decision. So I wrote to the vice-governor of Warsaw, Krevsky, who was married to the sister of a good friend of ours. He promised to give Lev a post as regional director. From that moment I decided to leave Tsarskoye Selo for ever and went to Kamenka with Aliona. In August 1903 we received a letter from Krevsky informing us that Lev had been named regional director for the Polish town of Wloclawek, in the province of Warsaw, one hour by road from the German border of Alexandrov/Thorn. Lev returned to Tsarskoye Selo in the autumn to relinquish his command and to pack our belongings.

Russian social life in a garrison town like Wloclawek was entirely new to me. All its principles, its views, its customs were the direct opposite of all I had seen until then. Most of the people were of very modest status, never left Wloclawek and mixed only with one another. Flirtations were common and went very far without causing either embarrassment or shame. Neither husbands nor wives paid any attention and their habits were extremely dissolute.


July 1905! Russia is drifting! Something is going wrong with the Russo-Japanese war. *Liberation* publishes articles that are increasingly fiery. Lev says that even in Wloclawek there are revolutionaries who are going around disseminating proclamations and calling for strikes.

One day the local factories went on strike and a crowd of workers marched on the town hall. Lev rode on his horse Vikhr into the crowd and tried to convince them to disperse, but nobody listened to him and the crowd grew larger. A detachment of soldiers, led by a young officer, appeared through the crowded streets.

The workmen, 5,000 of them, blocked the street for three whole days, during which the local citizens trembled for fear of brigandry. They finally came to an agreement with the factory managers, a resolution was passed that seemed to satisfy everyone, and the strike

*The aunts' house at Kamenka*

ended. A few days later Lev received a letter from the governor, congratulating him for having controlled the strike in such a diplomatic manner. This was most agreeable, and we decided there and then to go to Kamenka.


UNCLE NICHOLAS Vassilyevich lived in a house called the Green House, which stood in the middle of a small garden, and his two sisters, "the aunts", lived in another house where we were put up when we arrived from Wloclawek. Our description of the strike made a great impression on everyone. The aunts uttered ohs! and ahs!, and Uncle Nicholas repeatedly said, "Bravo! Bravo! So you were not scared! I am very pleased!"

However, the railroad strike that followed shook us. As our leave ended in October, we still hoped to return to Wloclawek by the last train before the strike. We were driven to the station in a carriage drawn by four white horses while Vassya, one of Lev's cousins, who was almost always drunk, galloped around the coach firing a revolver in the air. We were still some distance from the station when we saw the train was ready to leave. Vassya galloped off to make it wait for us; but fate willed otherwise. The train left without us and we had to return to Kamenka. (We learned a short time later that it had only been able to go as far as Brest, where it was forced to stop because the railway strike had begun!)

What luck that we had missed it! Furthermore, the next day Alionushka fell seriously ill. We were very worried about Lev's leave and feared it would not be extended. In the evenings we remained in the dining room watching Varya tie jampots while Tassya sewed a blouse, the sleeve of which she had accidentally cut off because she was so troubled by a telegram she received from her suitor Petya Ryjov.

During the three weeks we were forced to stay in Kamenka we received no letters or newspapers, and during those weeks our future was decided. Uncle Nicholas lost his two most faithful servants: the manager Gubert, who took another job, and the accountant Plessky, who, after working for Uncle Nicholas for over fifty years, was virtually abducted by the Davydoffs of Yurchikha. Thus Uncle Nicholas found himself alone. Lev suggested that he stay on to help him, to which the old man answered, "Thank you, Lev. Please do and get down to work right away!"

Ж. Д забастовка в Октябрь 1905 года в Каменкѣ.

Времяпрепровождение во время забастовки

*Sitting together in the kitchen at Kamenka waiting for news of the railway strike.*
*Tassya is sewing a blouse, Varvara is tying jam pots*

THE EXQUISITE LIFE that Kamenka had known when it was filled with people was a thing of the distant past. Its guiding spirit now was Uncle Nicholas. At 18 he had joined the Preobrazhensky Regiment and one day, during an important parade, the Emperor had noticed him as a new man and asked who he was. When told that it was Davydoff, son of the Decembrist exile, the Emperor said, "So that is why he stares at me like a wolf!" This remark so offended Uncle Nicholas, whose eyes were indeed serious and unsmiling, but who felt nothing but loyalty to the Tsar, that he resigned and retired to the country for good, in order to straighten out the estate that had been woefully neglected by his tutors during his minority. He finally made enough money to give each of his sisters and brothers (there were ten of them) a sum on which they could live. Most of them would come and stay in Kamenka as long as they wished, the married ones with their families.

Lev's father, Alexis Vassilyevich, who enjoyed the good life, had quickly spent his capital, so that his children had to be brought up mainly in Kamenka.

*The Decembrist's family returning from their Siberian exile in a "tarantass", a huge carriage which had difficulty climbing the steep hills*

THE AUNTS' HOUSE was a low, but quite large one-storey building with a green roof. The rooms were medium-sized but numerous and divided into two lots by a long corridor where later, during the long winter evenings, Lev and I liked to stroll while discussing the day's events.

At this time we occupied two tiny rooms in the left wing, where we worried about extended leave and dreamt of staying in Kamenka forever. Shivering in our cold beds, we asked ourselves what would happen if Lev stayed to run the estate and what Uncle Nicholas would do about his will.

When I became a part of Kamenka, Uncle Nicholas, Aunt Sasha, Aunt Lisa and Aunt Vera were living there. The aunts were educated ladies, quiet, kind and well brought up, who were always together, either sitting and reading or looking after sick peasants. Aunt Lisa, who was forceful and quick-tempered, would occasionally show her displeasure, but she was always fair and thoughtful. She loved her little dog, which she always held on her lap.

Aunt Sasha, the youngest of the three, remembered Siberia where she was born, and her father during his exile, whereas Aunt Lisa, who was born before her father was deported, had stayed in Russia. That is probably why Aunt Sasha had a somewhat sad look about her.

During the last years of his exile, her father Vassily Lvovich fell ill and became progressively weaker. Aunt Sasha would read to him. He was a very serious and intelligent man and he owned a large number of books that had been sent to him from Paris by his relatives the de Gramonts.

Aunt Sasha was very close to her parents. She was approximately 20 when her mother returned from Siberia with the children. Alexander II had amnestied the Decembrists when he became Tsar, but Vassily Lvovich died before this great day and the family left Krasnoyarsk without being aware of the amnesty. They only learned about it when, in one of the railway stations of Siberia, they ran into Prince Volkonsky, who was bringing the Tsar's manifesto, and this meeting was a very sad and touching one.


NICHOLAS VASSILYEVICH never married and never left Kamenka. He was a very robust man until he was 75. Short but thickset, he had severe eyes which frightened most people a little; but he spoke slowly and precisely in a pleasant and friendly tone of voice.

Though he never married he was not averse to mistresses; I was told that Ivan the gardener would act as his intermediary and bring home young girls. It was said that he had

*Uncle Nicholas with Aunt Sasha and Aunt Lisa; Lev and I are strolling in the corridor*

many children in the village, but he was always very generous with his mistresses when he left them and saw to it that they married well. In the last half of his life he lived with one of his laundresses, a beautiful Polish girl by whom he had a daughter, Varvara Nikolaevna, who went to live with her mother when she married. Later he had an affair with a girl who worked in the garden; she gave birth to a boy who died in infancy, and two girls, Nina Nikolaevna and Manya Nikolaevna.

At about this time one of Uncle Nicholas's brothers, Lev Vassilyevich, who had married Tchaikovsky's sister, Alexandra Ilyinishna, arrived in Kamenka and Uncle Nicholas took him on as manager of the estate. Alexandra Ilyinishna, a charming and endearing woman, had a great influence on her brother-in-law. Around 1873 her kindness and sympathy for him led her to try and build a family around him for his old age, and indeed she convinced him to adopt his eldest daughter Varvara Nikolaevna, and to install his last mistress and her daughters in more comfortable surroundings. This all happened, and of course it could not fail to scandalize certain members of the family, in particular Aunt Sasha. It was said that she never altogether forgave him. As long as Uncle Nicholas's affairs remained secret everyone was content, but when he installed his mistress openly for all to see, and went regularly to her home for tea at 5, it was not to be unexpected that everyone should feel outraged.

What pleasure it was for him to take tea in summer in the small wing of his mistress's house! Simple plates and a boiling samovar were set on the table. Standing in front of her master, the sweet and tender woman, with submissive blue eyes, would pour his tea. I can describe her because I was told that Nina looked like her.

When she was later married off, for reasons that I don't know, the two small girls moved into the big house to live with the aunts. Aunt Lisa took sides with Nicholas Vassilyevich and launched into the education of his daughters. A short while later they also took in Varvara Nikolaevna. The small house in the big garden was cleaned up, the office was moved there, and the children, who had forgotten their earlier life, became an integral part of Kamenka.

By 1899, when I arrived in Kamenka, Varvara and Nina had already married. Only Manya, frail and always ill, sad and discontented, never married, so she grew up without a name and no assurance of her future. It was only during our time there that Uncle Nicholas adopted her legally and gave her the name of Davydoff.

*Uncle Nicholas (with Lev at his side) and his three illegitimate daughters: Varvara, Manya and Nina*

THE PLESSKY AFFAIR concerns the Davydoff family who lived at Yurchikha, 3 versts from Kamenka. Uncle Nicholas's brother, Pyotr Vassilyevich, had had one son, Vassily Petrovich, who married Princess Olga Alexandrovna Lieven and lived in Yurchikha. They had three sons before Vassily died insane. His widow, an embittered woman, enormously fat, dark-skinned, mannish and rough, was devoted only to her sons Vassya, Petya and Sasha, and intended for one of them to inherit the whole Kamenka estate when Uncle Nicholas died. Aware of Plessky's influence on Uncle Nicholas, she built all her hopes on him to achieve her object, and she began to visit his office with noticeable frequency.

One day, when Lev was absent, she came to the office and a serious talk took place between her and Plessky. The latter got very excited, and when Lev arrived as the end of their conversation he was surprised to see Plessky twirling his cane in front of Olga Alexandrovna's nose and shouting, "I have a cane with two ends!" Olga Alexandrovna got up immediately with an outraged look and left the house. Lev had no idea what they had been arguing about, but did his best to calm Plessky down. Two or three hours later, however, two red-faced and grim-looking horsemen with whips in their hands appeared in Kamenka. They were Olga's sons Vassya and Petya. They went first to the office, but were told that Plessky was with Uncle Nicholas. They hurried over to the house and stood waiting in the courtyard. When Plessky eventually emerged from the house, they went up to him, one on each side, their whips twirling and whistling in the air. They told him in a nasty and menacing manner: "You are going to come with us right now and apologize to our mother for the horrid things you said to her this morning!"

The old man started to tremble at the thought of going into the den of these ruffians. His small grey beard shook and his face lost all its dignity and stoicism. He refused point blank to go with them, saying he had no reason to apologize, and walked off as fast as he could. He fled to the nearby aunts' house, but not before Petya's whip, whistling around his head, struck him painfully on the back. In a second he had disappeared inside the house and hid behind a screen near a wash-basin; sitting on the bidet, he never stopped howling.

The brothers dashed off furiously to the village where they managed to get roaring drunk. From time to time they returned to the house and bellowed for Plessky. It was not till 1 a.m. that Plessky decided to rise from the bidet, ordered us to take some pikes which the guards used and accompany him to the room by the kitchen. The next morning when Lev went to see how he had spent the night, he was nowhere to be found. At 4 in the morning he had ordered the four-horse coach to be got ready, and had been driven to the station, not at Kamenka but at Raygorod. There he disappeared completely and for ever!

*Poor terrified Plessky, barely able to walk, as we prop him up and carry protective pikes in our hands*

WHEN LEV TOOK OVER management of the estate, it was divided into three farming enterprises: the Nikolaevsky, the Pliakovsky and the Podlesnoe, which included the Lesnichestva and comprised some 2,000 *dessiatines*. Everything was in perfect condition but run in a rather old-fashioned way. Lev started making his way modestly. He had a great deal of patience and intuition. In the office he listened to the old servants, learning and informing himself from them.

At the end of October the railway strike came to an end and we left by the first available train for Wloclawek, Lev to settle his affairs and Tassya and I to gather our effects and furniture and send them to Kamenka.

On the long journey we arrived one day at noon at a village where we were supposed to have lunch and feed the horses. We walked into an inn, all dark and warm inside. We ordered a samovar, which in no time at all was steaming and singing on our table. The door opened softly and the yellowish and taciturn face of the innkeeper appeared. He asked us if we wished to hear a harpist who sang traditional Polish songs. The musician was a little old man with thick hair as light and soft as a swan's feathers, clean-shaven except for a moustache. We ate and drank while he played and sang for us. I don't remember ever having heard anything more poetic and original. His old fingers were still able to pluck the strings with agility and his cracked, frail voice expressed a whole range of emotions.

When it was time to move on, the harpist followed us out of the inn, raising his hat every minute and thanking us with a winning smile for the generosity of our tip.

During our brief stay in Wloclawek, which was virtually in a state of war, Lev was able to resign his post, and Tassya and I packed all our belongings. Finally, on 30 November 1905, we were back in peaceful, beloved Kamenka, our new home.

UPON OUR RETURN from Wloclawek, we had to borrow money immediately. The house that had been allotted to us was called the "doctorate" and stood right by the wall of the big courtyard on the other side of the road – in truth, in the village itself. We moved in just before Christmas and furnished the house with the shipment that had arrived from Wloclawek.

When we went to have tea with the aunts, Lev carried Alionushka in his arms. She wore a hat that covered her ears, and red mittens. In the aunts' living room it was warm and cosy.

*Having a meal at an inn on our way back to Wloclawek,*
*and listening to an old harpist playing traditional Polish airs*

*Tea with the aunts. Bread is being toasted on the grate and the samovar is steaming away.*

*Grigory takes Lev's coat as he comes in out of the cold.*

We were greeted on our arrival by Grigory, the elder of the menservants (there was another one named Feodor) and he took our coats. In the drawing room a samovar was boiling on a round table covered with a cloth. There was a cake, fresh brioches and buns with jam. In one corner a fire burned in the fireplace and Aunt Sasha poured the tea. Manya, one of Uncle Nicholas's three illegitimate daughers, took Alionushka on her lap and offered her a brioche, but she made a fuss and stretched her arms out to me.

Manya said that Uncle wanted to give us a cow. I flushed with pleasure. We drank tea. Everyone was gay and happy.

A T FIRST our modest, even poor, house seemed strange to us, but very quickly we grew accustomed to it and indeed came to like it precisely because of its modesty, which cancelled all materialistic considerations. It was evidence of a contempt for all that was petty and mean; and everything in Kamenka was so real and virtuous that its inhabitants, its servants and its guests, seemed to form an indestructible entity. The other Davydoffs, those of Yurchikha and Verbovka, had become civilized in the empty sense of the word; they had good beds and had arranged their houses in a modern way, according to what was in fashion, but Kamenka itself remained as Uncle Nicholas had found it in the first half of the nineteenth century.

Uncle Nicholas came to see our house. Striking the floor with his feet and his cane, he asked if I was pleased and apologized for the fact that everything was in such poor condition.

Everything seemed marvellous to us as winter set in. Lev earned 250 roubles a month plus our living expenses. We had hired a young girl named Dunya and had also brought a cook from Matussov by the name of Ivan Novokhatko, who reigned over a rather dark kitchen that was full of smoke.

*My kitchen at Kamenka, in the charge of our chef, Ivan Novokhatko*

THICK SNOW is falling now. In two days' time it will be Christmas Eve. There is a smell of snow and frost. The pine trees and the shrubs around the house are like blue porcelain. Today I will go to the woods with Lev to find a buck. We must have a good roast for the festivities.

After lunch, a "grinjal", a low sleigh with wider runners used to transport heavy goods in winter, is driven up in front of the porch of the big house. Lev and I sit down in it. Over my pelisse I put a "burka", a Caucasian felt coat, which belongs to Uncle Nicholas, and Lev wears his bearskin coat. The footmen stick pieces of fur in the corners to add warmth, and we are off! Alionushka looks through the window and claps her hands on the pane.

We pass below Yurchikha, then along undulating hills. Close to the Podlesnoe farm we climb up by a lane into peaceful white forest. From time to time a lump of snow falls from a branch and softly strikes us.

Lev has moved his legs out of the lambskins and has loaded his gun. We keep a look out for spoor on the fresh snow. Here are rabbit tracks and there are the small triangular markings of birds, and further on we see where a fox has passed. And now we hear a dull sound and in front of us a buck trots by. Lev trembles but does not raise his gun. Sidor, the coachman, has also reacted and smiles.

We glide on slowly, looking right and left, and suddenly Sidor pulls up the horses and points with his whip to the right. Lev jumps from the sleigh and hides behind a large oak tree. We move slowly forward; there, about forty paces ahead of us, stands a stag, its head with beautiful antlers raised high, following the horses with its eyes. A shot rings out and the beast makes two or three bounds forward before crashing to the ground.

I close my eyes. I hate hunting. I hold the reins while Sidor and Lev run to their prey and drag the stag by its hind legs to the sleigh.

"Let's go for a ride in the forest," says Lev. "It's still early."

*Lev shooting a stag. I remain on the sleigh and our coachman Sidor holds the reins*

ALREADY ON THE MORNING of Christmas Eve the fir tree has been brought into the dining room. We keep Alionushka in the drawing room so that she will not see us decorating it. Its scent spreads through the whole house and I set fire on purpose to a few small branches so that the smell of Christmas may be everywhere. The tree has been set in the corner near the window and its dark branches stand out against the snowy background.

I hang up golden nuts that I have been painting all week. The gold sparkles as if the nuts were alive. Here are the Crimean apples with their red cheeks; they hang heavily at the tip of the branches. We tie on tangerines. In Kamenka all the fruits, sweets, chocolate, anything can be found in the Jewish shops.

It is freezing, about -10°C! The aunts have arrived and are playing with Alionushka in the drawing room. Lev and I light the tree and open wide the doors that give on to the corridor. Alionushka enters, holding the hand of Sasha Novokhatko, the cook's son, and she looks wide-eyed at the tree, the miracle-tree. Behind her come the aunts, and then the nursemaid, Anna Nikolaevna, who is the daughter of the aunts' housekeeper.

Sasha looks at the tree without saying a word or smiling, while Alionushka claps her hands, whistles and covers him in paper wrappings.


CHRISTMAS ON THE ESTATE is an occasion of joy. The snow crackles under the shoes of the women and the children all dressed in their Sunday best. They stand by their men, their faces painted with ochre or black soot or simply with chalk, stuffing themselves with food and behaving naughtily while the sun sinks into the scarlet snow as if it were on fire.

Soon the meadows will empty, the fires will be lit in the *khatkas* – the Ukrainian peasant homes – and Christmas Eve will start with the ringing of the church bells calling the faithful to mass.

*The decorated Christmas tree in the aunts' dining room*

*Christmas dinner: Uncle Nicholas, the aunts, Lev, Alionushka and I*

*The aunts going off to mass on Christmas Eve*

CHRISTMAS WAS FOR ME the best time of the year, the most intimate, the cosiest, especially that first year in Kamenka when the revolution was spreading and the whole of Russia was erupting with riots, strikes and demonstrations.

At that time there lived in Kamenka a notary, a certain Dolenga-Semenovsky, a very able, decided, intelligent and energetic man, in spite of his unprepossessing looks. He had a hard face with large, cruel and searching eyes. He spoke in a manner that brooked no discussion.

One day when he was chatting with Lev, Dolenga-Semenovsky asked, ''Who is Nicholas Vassilyevich's heir?'' Lev answered that for the time being nothing had been decided, and he told him the story of the exiled Decembrist grandfather, the fact that only the children born

84

*Uncle Nicholas and the notary Dolenga-Semenovsky discussing Uncle's will*

after the marriage of their parents before the exile were entitled to an inheritance, that is, Pyotr and Nicholas. If the latter did not make a will, the sole legal heirs would be the three brothers in Yurchikha. Dolenga said, "Oh no! The inheritance should be yours because you work here and are so close to him."

Lev did not believe Uncle Nicholas would ever bring himself to do that. But the fiery Dolenga-Semenovsky was determined to persuade him. Uncle Nicholas hummed and hawed: "Yes, I wanted to leave everything to my brother Alexey but he died . . ."

"You must do something because the people at Yurchikha are dangerous," said Dolenga, getting very excited and using colourful language.

A little while later he came back to the subject but Uncle Nicholas could only answer, "I have done nothing but think about it."

"You should leave everything to Lev Alexeyevich," insisted Dolenga. "You like him and he will not abandon Kamenka, he will not offend anyone, and he will continue to live here as you have done."

And so it came about, in early February 1906, that Uncle Nicholas signed a will in favour of Lev Alexeyevich Davydoff.

THE EVENING AFTER Dolenga brought us the news about Uncle Nicholas's will, we could not sleep for ages. Lev was almost stunned, but gathered up his courage to keep from showing anything because Uncle Nicholas had asked that no one be told.

Our household was blossoming. We had a first-class cook in Novokhatko. I myself took care of the dairy products. I prepared a wonderful fresh cream which people would come and regale themselves on. One day at the market Lev bought me a pedigree pig, a sow with an upturned nose, for 25 roubles. I called it Matriochka. We loved to walk through the market. It started next to our fence, to which the muzhiks would tie their carts and stalls. The Jewish shops swarmed with people. Crowds filled the street where Jewish vendors sold horses and calves.

February ends and March is here. The months, with their change of weather suddenly breaking the rhythm of our life, start to whisper in our ears, "Spring! Spring!" The days grow longer, the sun shines through the windows and warms our rooms. The larks start to sing, the snow has melted in the fields, the sowers have begun their work on the still wet soil and are followed by the harrows. On March 9th we go out in a drozhky in spite of the mud, to see how the sowing is proceeding. It is warm in the carriage which Sidor drives as in winter.

When we return home, boiling tea is awaiting us near the fireplace in the aunts' house, and we warm our frozen hands by the fire while we tell them what we have been doing.

24

*In early spring Lev and I go out in a drozhky to watch the sowing*

HOLY WEEK IS FILLED with all sorts of events. People hasten to the church while in the kitchen and bakeries the Easter cakes and brioches are rising. Housewives kneeling piously for the service think, "Oh, I haven't yet strained the white cheese for the paskha!"

On Thursday people get busy in the larder, the bakery and the kitchen. Pounds and pounds of flour are spread on the boards, on tables and in basins. Hundreds of eggs are broken. Sugar is poured without being measured. Almonds, raisins, saffron, nutmeg are added.

With Alionushka I gaze at all this and delightedly breathe the fragrant fumes, because today we fast, and everywhere in the house and in the courtyard there is the smell of sunflower oil . . . We go with the housekeeper to the larder, where she shows us the paskhas and the painted eggs that have been prepared for the servants. Alionushka jumps on the weighing machine and swings herself.

*Preparations for Easter. Alionushka and I with the housekeeper in the larder.*
*Each servant will receive one paskha and a dozen painted eggs*

THE DAY BEFORE EASTER, on Passion Sunday, at 9 a.m. in the big house, after a short grace at the buffet, a priest blessed the paskhas that the servant brought in, and for the first time sang "Kristos Voskresse!" (Christ is risen!) Aunt Sasha, who fasted during the whole of Lent, raised her face adoringly towards the priest and a great joy shone in her eyes.

After blessing the Easter fare, Father Dimitry removed his mitre and paid his respects to the aunts, inviting them to go to church for the Easter service.

All who were able to go put on white dresses, and the children stuck flowers and a mass of ribbons in their hair. The little country church became alive with the gay chatter of people. Though it was barely 100 feet from our house, we always took the coach to go there. It was all lit up, and in the still moist grass around it oil lamps burned with bright and smoky flames. We remained standing throughout the service but returned home before mass. There awaiting us were the traditional coffee and paskha, cake and the rest of the Easter fare.

*Father Dimitry blessing the Easter table*

SPRING ADVANCES by rapid stages. Every day in every farm, things are moving and progressing. Temporary workers are hired, cattle are inventoried, the worthless animals are eliminated. Everyone is busy in the office. Here are the two stewards, all red from the wind. The old gamekeeper is there too, as well as the old manager of the sugar factory. They are all there standing around Uncle Nicholas and Lev.

Alionushka, Anna Nikolaevna and I go for a walk in the garden, still wearing our winter coats, and pick crocuses, those dark lilac-coloured flowers, the first to bloom after the snow melts. How they smell of honey! After them, small blue asters break out in masses all along the fence through the old leaves under the trees, and when the sun becomes warmer it will be the turn of the pale violets way down at the bottom of the garden.

What delight! The garden covered 10–15 *dessiatines*, almost all on a slope that dropped down to the Tiasmin river. I have never seen so many flowering lilac trees anywhere else. There were simple ones, pedigree, mossy, Persian ones, pink ones, every sort one could imagine. In early April we would walk as if bewitched by this mass of colours, which we never had enough of, especially if they had been dampened by a warm spring shower. We walked down moist lanes between lawns that were beginning to look green. We sat on a bench while Alionushka ran down the lanes with one of the dachshunds.

*The lilacs in the large garden at Kamenka*

THE SUMMER OF 1906 was a troubled one. Various rumours were circulated. At one moment, people said that a family of landowners had been locked into their country house and burnt alive by the muzhiks. Another time we heard that a steward's cottage had been burned down. When a fire was detected in the neighbourhood, the churches rang the tocsin. Sometimes we heard them ringing all night, close by or far away and all of us rushed to the fire to see how the wind was tearing away burning hay and blowing it over to the village, thus starting new fires.

Our turn came. One afternoon at 2 o'clock a horseman rode over from Podlesnoe to tell us that the farm was on fire. This was our first serious alarm. Lev and I rushed over to the stables which were on the other side of the road, seized the horses and sped to the scene of the fire. On the road we were overtaken by the intendant Varvashin, who was also on his way to Podlesnoe, so we jumped into his drozhky and went with him.

The long stable, flanked by stalls for eighty oxen, with a pigsty next to it and a larder — everything was on fire. It was obvious that, during the lunchtime break, someone had set fire to the side that overlooked the fields. The water hose was already in action; firemen from other villages arrived and helped to extinguish the fire. Lev and I ran among the embers and threw out those that were still burning. Thank God, none of the cattle had been burnt, and the damage was limited to the thatched roof. The brick walls had resisted.

*Rushing to the fire at Podlesnoe*

THE FIELDS WERE COVERED with almost ripe golden wheat. For a long time Lev and Varvashin had been discussing the harvesting with Uncle Nicholas, but a sort of malaise reigned in the office. Varvashin and the steward said that the peasants were demanding an extra sheaf and simply strolled around refusing to go to work, preferring to make trouble in the village and to act in a threatening manner. The men in the office didn't know what to do.

The first day of harvesting arrived, but no workmen appeared. On the second and third days, there were still no workers. The muzhiks said that they would start harvesting only if they were given what they had asked for. The state of tension having reached its peak, Lev asked his cousin Mitya to cable the governor for a detachment of dragoons.

Huge crowds assembled near the town hall (at that time Kamenka had around 8,500 inhabitants, two churches and two rural districts) and waited. The day came when the dragoons were supposed to arrive, and a group of us went out to greet them. Malevolent and treacherous faces stared at us as we walked through the village. In a little while a torrential rain fell on us with thunder and lightning. We remained standing stoically, drenched and dirtied by the mud, our hair hanging down our noses! Suddenly, from behind the rise, we saw arriving down the road the detachment of dragoons with an officer at their head, all singing a marching song. We shouted enthusiastically, and when the smart soldiers in their white shirts passed in front of us, we hugged the necks of their horses.

The wheat was ripe and had been flattened by the torrential rain, so it had to be harvested at all costs. That evening, when we had dinner with the aunts, everyone was calm. Uncle didn't even mention the events that were taking place.

On our way home in the dark night, we found everything silent and empty. Tonight we could sleep peacefully: the dragoons were keeping watch. But in the middle of the night I was suddenly wakened by the ringing of the tocsin in both churches. From far off we could hear faintly the sounds of rioting, voices, the stamping of a horse's hoofs. Quickly the sounds came closer and a horseman was slapping at our door with his whip. "I have come to fetch Lev Alexeyevich!" he shouted. "The Nikolaevsky farm is on fire!" Lev seemed to dress in a matter of seconds and dashed from the house.

It was not until morning that he returned and described the ugly situation that had developed between the dragoons and the peasants. The commanding officer of the detachment had ordered that the instigators of the fire be brought to him; when there was no response to this, he had decided to requisition the peasants — that is, to feed his men and

*The arrival of the dragoons*

horses at their expense. Soldiers had therefore been despatched to the villages to take all they could lay their hands on – cattle, bread, grain, milk, butter.

We were extremely worried and Lev went over to see the officer in charge to ask him to put an end to this affair. He argued that relations with the peasants were already very difficult and that such a measure could only make matters worse. Nevertheless, it continued until evening and only ended the following morning, when the stewards and the authorities went to call the men to work at 4 a.m., saying they could have the extra sheaf.

The dragoons stayed a few more days, then left when the fields were filled with people, as in more peaceful times. We were sorry to see them go, and also a little afraid.

THE DISAGREEMENT having been settled, the gathering of the wheat has begun. We walk around the farms and admire how each day the haystacks grow on the large fields. The sun is warm. It is early July. The peasants have started taking the third sheaf. Their stacks rise as high as houses.

It is almost noon and the women have already stopped work. One is feeding her newborn baby. Another is sleeping peacefully under a tent made of rags tied to three posts to protect her from the sun.

After gazing at all this, we return home in a cabriolet driven by Lev. At home borscht awaits us, with pork, tomatoes, kasha, delicious fresh kvass, roast chicken and ice cream.

*The harvesting of the wheat*

THE SUN GOES DOWN. A purple light sets the horizon aflame. There is not a cloud in the sky. In the afternoon the temperature has risen to 26°C in the shade. No one has ventured out of the house before 5 but now everyone is outside. The young women gardeners hitch up their skirts above their knees and water the plants abundantly with water taken from the barrels where it has warmed up all day. Ivan, uncle's gardener, supervises the work. He is a bald, not very tall man with a sly expression. He has six young assistants who, in the evening, water the plants that wilt under the stifling heat. Ivan attaches a great deal of importance to the flower beds and always makes a point of being present when they are watered.

At sunset I take Alionushka to the aunts' house and play with her in the small garden, breathing that wonderful atmosphere of wet grass. Soon Anna Nikolaevna takes away my little girl for her nap while we remain with the aunts on the terrace. Glass candlesticks stand on the table and the whole household arrives: Sasha, Vera, Nina, Katya, Shura, Manya, Varya, Minya Romanovna, Verochka who has just finished the Institute, and her brother Kolya Sandberg who is a student. The young ones are discreetly silent. Uncle chats with Lev. We have meat cutlets with a raisin sauce, and rice pudding with fresh cream. The samovar boils at one end of the table and Aunt Sasha pours tea into drinking glasses.

Turning to me she says: "Our food must not seem very good to you. I hear you have a good cook," and she laughs guiltily.

Indeed their cook, Jacob, is as old as he is bad. He prepares what he likes and in whatever way he feels like doing it. Usually for lunch he prepares a soup, a very light, liquid soup. It would be all right if it were borscht but it is only a liquid bouillon, which is strange because he is allotted one pound of meat per person, rice and vermicelli. This is followed by roast chicken or by a lean fillet that is rather old and bloodless, with spinach or peas. Dessert consists of cake, jelly or blancmange, several types of preserves, and in summer a fruit macedoine in a watermelon. Fortunately the products are fresh because Jacob is anything but a chef and has no culinary talent whatsoever . . .

68

*Uncle Nicholas's garden in the heat of summer*

*The opening of the hunting season in September*

THE OPENING of the hunting season took place in September. It was Yuri, who lived with Uncle Nicholas's permission in a smallholding next to the Big Wood, that usually organized the hunts, but this year Lev has taken over. He has invited the neighbours, and early one morning, Lev's brother Grisha and our cousin Kolya Sandberg go to the meeting place in the forest. The ladies meet them at twelve for lunch.

The hunting season signifies the beginning of a new era for the village. It marks the end of agricultural activities, the end of summer and the prospect of the unique autumn of Little Russia.

It is still very warm in the first half of September, but the light has already changed. At 10 a.m. the carriage appears which will convey the lunch, the samovar, the cooks and the servants to the forest clearing. We follow at 11, in summer dresses with scarves around our heads, a fashion I have introduced in place of town hats.

The meeting place is a clearing with fresh green grass that has grown after the dry spell in the autumnal dampness. The horses are unharnessed and start grazing right away. A barrel of water is installed and the carriages are placed in the shade. In the centre of the clearing the hunters' table is set up with mounds of straw around it for seats.

The carriages with the hunters arrive, their rifles smelling of powder. Lev shouts, "Grigory, bring the glasses!" Everyone moves towards the table, vodka flows, glasses clink. Grigory hurriedly brings the zakusky, and the famished hunters grab at them while the dead animals are taken out of the carriages and lined up on the ground. The lunch menu is always the same: zakusky, vodka, borscht with pirozhky, mutton or another meat stew, biscuits, fruit and of course several sorts of wine.

AUTUMN ARRIVED, and even though the days were still warm we sealed up the windows and doors to keep the cold out of the house. Manya already muffled herself up in shawls. Her nose had gone red and her lips were dry and cracked.

Poor Manya had been convinced after many years to go and see her unmarried mother, who lived quietly in the village. She continued to see her occasionally, and when the woman died, she was buried in the church cemetery. From then on Manya visited the grave regularly. Manya had made a good and kind gesture towards her mother, particularly as they did not meet on the same footing, Manya having been brought up in gentility and her mother a servant.

*Cold weather returns. Manya, who particularly feels the cold, is huddled in shawls. Aunt Lisa wears an eyeshade because she is sensitive to light*

THE RAINS HAVE STARTED and there is frost in the morning. The village is all dark and only the shop windows throw a pale light outside as the doors are tightly closed.

Small low Jewish shops line both sides of the long paved street that divides the village in two. The Jews sell everything – wool, cotton, material of all sorts, cheviot, taffeta, moiré, as well as haberdashery, wine, fruits. The inhabitants of Kamenka and the neighbouring villages, the landowners and the workers on the estate, all go to the Jewish shops. They can find saddles, rope, soap, perfume, pencils, crockery, suet, nails, barrels of oil, furniture, kerosene, candles, light bulbs – anything you care to name.

If you walked into a fabric shop, three or four attendants would pounce on you, and you couldn't possibly leave without their showing you everything that was in the shop. "You don't need to show me all that," we would say, "we haven't come for that today."

"Sit down, please," the owner would say, pushing forward a chair. "It is only to show you. You don't need to buy."

"All I want is some nainsook," I would say, and he answered, "We have some. Of course we have some. But look at this!" He unrolled a marvellous dark blue woollen cloth. "It has just arrived. Take it for a dress. You will be delighted with it."

"It is very nice, but today I only want some nainsook."

"What about this?" and he would throw a bright green Liberty print onto the counter. "But nainsook . . . ?"

"Yes, yes, here is some nainsook. Moshe! Cut one arshin of nainsook!" And while Moshe cuts the nainsook, the sales talk goes on and on.

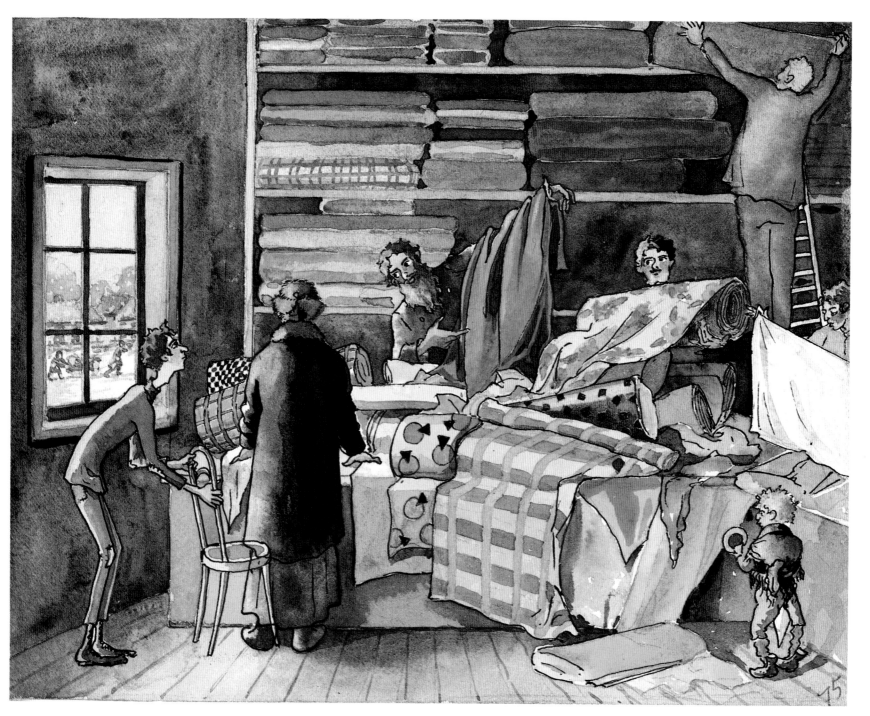

*The Jewish fabric shop in Kamenka village*

THE BIG FAIR in Zlatopol took place during October. Zlatopol was a large village, much larger than Kamenka. Each year we needed horses and oxen for the estate. Lev and I decided to go there with Sarancha, our experienced manager, to learn how to buy and not to be cheated.

We rode into Zlatopol at noon. The enormous square was completely occupied by the fair. We edged our way through the carts and the cattle, and stopped near the centre. Sarancha descended from our cart and disappeared. The gypsies and the Jews were running in every direction and showing off their horses. A muzhik slapped a Jew's hand after haggling over a horse.

After a lunch of pirozhky, salami and wine, we went nosing around. What noise! What commotion! We ran into an argument between two gypsies and had no notion what it was all about.

One shouted to Lev, "Here, hold these horses for me! I was just saying to him – "

People were trying to move me away from Lev, who was saying, "But I don't want your old nags!"

The others started shouting even louder while pinning us more and more. Lev was reaching into his pocket for some money; the gypsies became more agitated, and another one joined in.

"Just lend me 100 roubles for one minute! I only want to hold it in my hand!"

"Don't give it to him! He's a crook!"

I was gripped by such a feeling of terror that I grabbed Lev's sleeve and tugged to get him away from there. I was certain this was all a trap, a comedy acted out to rob us. Sarancha knew all these tricks and had tried several times to extricate us, but the people, all of them brigands, prevented him. We finally got away with difficulty, and the whole band dispersed at once.

Sarancha managed to buy a pair of oxen. Together we bought a dozen horses two hours later, and after tying their bridles to our cart we set off for home.

*Lev and I among the crowd at the fair in Zlatopol*

WINTER AGAIN! I don't know how the others felt, but as for me, my heart thumped and my soul trembled when I thought of snow. Of course the winter was long and often harsh. For people who lived in poor northern villages far from any railway, buried under masses of snow in primitive homes miles away from all other people, six or seven months of winter were not easy to endure. But in Kamenka, only 2 versts by paved road from the railway, living on a lovely estate among neighbours, and Kiev within easy reach, it was quite another matter.

On a day when everything is covered in snow, we go to the Podlesnoe farm which we love so much. New roofs have been built since the fire, and even the small barns are ready. It is a pleasure to see how the buildings have improved.

*Podlesnoe farm in the winter*

77

At 4 p.m. it is time to go home. As the horses trot off joyfully, snow begins to fall. It crackles under the runners of our sleigh. White frost covers Lev's moustache and beard. The road passes alongside a frozen pond, and here are the first houses of Yurchikha. The snow-covered horses slow down to a walk, but the snow falls even harder. When we leave Yurchikha, the wind catches us and raises snow from the fields, dry as sand. We can't see anything; the horizon is invisible behind the milky haze.

"Where are we?" Lev asks Sidor. "You've turned around."

"No, I am on the right road," Sidor answers.

"We are in a field!" I shout, and a strange anxiety grips us as we realize we have lost our way. No trace of a road can be seen or heard under the horses' hoofs.

Sidor finally admits that he has lost his way, but he is confident the horses will take us home.

Suddenly something dark passes in front of us. Sidor cries out, "Hey! Is this the road to Kamenka?"

"Yes," answers a muffled voice.

"Right or left?"

"Left for Kamenka," and the ghostly presence vanishes.

A quarter of an hour later we see the dark grey houses of our village.


The blizzard continued all night, covering the balcony and the windows with snow. In the morning we woke to the sound of shovels digging us out. In every house stoves crackled and were heated to the maximum. The winter scents of burning and smoke were everywhere.

Alionushka was already dressed and climbed on the window sill. We both admired the view from there. What a fall of snow there had been! Blue trenches ran through the immaculate whiteness under the shovel of Bolitsky and the other workmen.

*Lost in the snow*

*Digging out after the blizzard*

I ASKED FOR the snow to be swept off a large section of the pond below the garden, and I went ice-skating there every day. Alionushka came to slide on the ice and ride in a sleigh. On the other side of the pond one could see the smoke and hear the noise of our sugar factory and even smell the pressed beets. On the bridge over the Tiasmin passed long files of ox-drawn carts carrying the pressed beets from the Nikolaevsky farm and horse-drawn carts taking away the bales of sugar from the courtyard.

ONE OF THE WINTER pastimes I invented was to ride in a sleigh drawn by dogs. Manya had a collie named Orlik which had had two little bitches by a curly-haired mongrel. These two large and hairy beasts, Lissa and Latochka, were therefore half pedigreed. I had the idea of harnessing them to a light sleigh that I had bought. On calm winter days Tolya, the twelve-year-old son of Anna Feodorovna, Alionushka and I would go riding and, in order to make the bitches run (they had never been trained), we tied pieces of meat on the end of a long whip and they would try to catch them, running as fast as they could, thus conveying us at top speed along the snow-packed alleys.

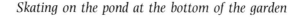
*Skating on the pond at the bottom of the garden*

*Riding in a sleigh drawn by two dogs*

*1906 – Christmas at the Donats'*

EDWARD FEODOROVICH DONAT started his career in Kamenka as a young and well-educated trainee. He came from an excellent family, not Germans but rather Germanized Balts. At university he studied agronomy, and before graduating he had to undertake a practical training course. It was then that he became steward at Podlesnoe. He married a charming young girl, Lydia Anatolyevna, from his social set, and was promoted to the post of manager. After spending a few years in Kamenka, he became the manager of Gruchevsk, a nearby estate owned by relatives called Bobrinsky, but he remained on friendly terms with Kamenka. Once upon a time Gruchevsk had belonged to the Davydoffs, but one of the Decembrist's brothers, a notorious gambler, had lost it to his neighbour Bobrinsky.

The Donats' home was gay and hospitable, always filled with charming young people. In 1906 we spent Christmas with them. Their two lovely daughters and a number of cousins delighted us all with dancing and games. It was that day that I heard for the first time, spoken by the young Donat cousins, new revolutionary expressions such as "arbitrary decisions", "the right to freedom of speech", that seemed out of place in this warm atmosphere of comfort and refinement.

During the summer of 1908, Volodya Krassovsky, one of Lev's former comrades-in-arms, came to visit us and complained about the way his estate in the province of Kherson was being mismanaged. He was in any case bored on his remote estate, and we suggested that he sell it and buy something in our neighbourhood. Close to Kamenka lived a widower who was no longer young and had grown-up sons. When he remarried a younger woman and had a son by her, he decided to sell his estate, Dubrova, in order to assure their financial future.

Krassovsky, Lev and I drove over to see the owner of Dubrova. No sooner had we driven into the forest than we were seized by a feeling of delight and charmed by the wonderful scents that emanated from it.

The house was not very large, only one storey high, and a bit pretentious-looking with urns on the roof and a terrace that gave onto the wood. The owner greeted us in a friendly fashion and showed us around the house, the farm and the park. I walked as if in a trance. Though I kept praising it to Krassovsky, I felt a terrible envy gnawing away at my heart, and I almost cried at the thought that we could not buy it ourselves.

Krassovsky was happy to buy it, but was not able to do so before selling his own estate. Lev offered to put up the deposit for him, and that was done not long after our visit. But the thought of Dubrova would not leave me in peace. I would say to Lev, "Why don't you buy it yourself? Does Krassovsky really need such a big estate? He is alone. He will not really live there!"

In January, when the deed of sale was to be signed, Krassovsky wrote to Lev to say that he had not been able to raise the money and had given up the idea of buying Dubrova. With tears in my eyes I begged Lev to buy it. He had to think it over in his logical and rational way. Money was required. He asked advice of those whose opinion he respected . . . Finally he reached the decision to borrow the money from Kamenka and buy Dubrova in my name! When he settled the whole thing he was beaming. "All is well," he said, "Dubrova is ours. You may settle there whenever you wish!"

DURING THAT 1908/09 WINTER we suddenly decided to go abroad. We had not left Kamenka for three years. Uncle Nicholas was his usual kind self when he gave his blessing to our trip to Nice.

It was an interesting journey. There were snowstorms in Italy, so strong that we reached Genoa only with great difficulty and nine hours late. We had to stop there because the train went no further.

After a bad night in Genoa, we went on to Nice, where the weather was clear and warm, the air fragrant with the scent of flowers. We stayed at the Hotel Splendide on the rue Victor Hugo, where we had large rooms, light and warm.

Two months in Nice did wonders for my health and spirits.


ON THE WAY HOME from Nice, we stopped off in Brittany to see my sister Juliet and her husband Georges Courtin. After all the sun and heat of the Riviera, Moros, the château where they lived near Concarneau, seemed damp and ugly with its humid rooms, its icy cold sheets and the continuous rain.

But we were homesick by now and my heart grew lighter as we started on the long journey back to Kamenka. On the final lap, there was rain turning to hail, then snow. Where was the sun of Nice? Something warmer than the Riviera sun filled my heart as I saw the Pliakovsky stream. The train began to brake down the hill side. We were ready, standing by the exit. When the train stopped, we could see the stationmaster on the platform with his red cap and his collar turned up; and the servants were all turning their backs to the wind.

We hurled ourselves out of the carriage. Grigory and the groom were there with the horse cart for the luggage. We were caught by the storm and I threw myself at Alionushka and wrapped her up in my plaid.

After a wild drive through the snow, we stopped at the aunts' house to have a cup of coffee with them. Aunt Sasha, Aunt Lisa, Aunt Katya and Aunt Vera were all standing at the windows. On the porch we were grabbed again by the snowstorm, but in the hallway it was warm, the stoves were going full blast.

We were home again.

*Our departure in the snow for Nice*

# 3 Dubrova, War and Revolution

It was not till the end of April that we moved to Dubrova. We took the entire staff with us. We bought a cow, and all the food was brought from Kamenka.

A young soldier, highly recommended, was named steward. He was first sent to the Nikolaevsky farm to learn the job, but he created such a good impression right from the start that Lev had no hesitation in naming him steward of Dubrova. He came from Moldavia and was a very handsome man. His name was Yaposkurt.

The animals were in poor condition and we set at once to renew the stock. We inspected our new possessions on a hot May day, and not the smallest spot went unexamined. The trough for the cattle near the well, the large enclosures, the barns, the servants' quarters, everything was wonderful.

There was an 80-*dessiatine* park separated by a ditch from our land on one side, and on the other from that of our neighbours, the Rogovskis, who were Polish. I loved to sit on the edge of that ditch and look in the distance at what seemed to be blue sea. That particular spot was called "the three oak trees", because three very thick oak trees grew there, covered by large stag beetles.

We put everything we had into Dubrova, all our hearts, our tastes and our creative spirit.

Soon after we moved to Dubrova we got to know a charming family called Szymanowski, who owned a small estate Tymoshovka not far from Verbovka. The Szymanowskis had two sons, Felix, who was a pianist, and Karol, a composer, and there were three daughters. Their house was large, with a garden that sloped down gently towards a pond.

Sometimes when we visited them, only a small group of neighbours were there, and then Karol or Felix would sit at the piano and offer us sublime moments which I will never forget.

*The "three oak trees" at Dubrova*

*A musical evening at the Szymanowskis'*

The "uninitiated" went to the billiard room and played there, while in the semi-darkness of the drawing room, lit by only one kerosene lamp, we listened in rapt silence. Through one of the open windows we could see under the starry sky the dark outline of the pine trees that grew right next to the house, and through another, small flowering heads and lazy Glories of Dijon that climbed up the side of the house. Felix became another person when he sat at the piano and played a moving and tortured Chopin *Ballade* or Schumann's *Carnaval*. As for Karol, he seemed to become immaterial as his beautiful hands moved over the keyboard creating sounds that were not of this earth.

It was only when the "uninitiated" returned to the drawing room and announced that the horses were ready, that one's dream was shattered.

OUR SECOND SUMMER at Dubrova was a particularly hot one. At the end of the day, as evening started to fall, we would get ready to go somewhere, for instance to pick flowers or gather mushrooms in the forest, but one time we decided to fish for freshwater crayfish in the pond. The evening was bewitching, and I ordered the coach to be harnessed as well as the cart for our cook Ivan, because we had decided to eat out in the open air.

We settled ourselves near the pond, tied small pieces of meat at the end of lines and plunged them into the water. Very soon we caught enormous crayfish that lived on the sandy bottom. We had taken with us Aniuta, our clever and resourceful chambermaid, who stepped into the water naked and caught crayfish with her hands after searching for them on the muddy bottom. Alexander Mikhailovich Boborikin, the notary who had handled the Dubrova deed of sale, sat close to the edge of the pond, on a small folding stool, and gazed with delight at her fishing and even more at the graceful shape of Aniuta's breasts, which would pop every minute in and out of the water as she lifted her hand holding a crayfish.

A bonfire had been lit on the embankment and its flames rose lively and gay, their reflection in the water resembling red serpents. The cook had started to prepare the first pot of water and he set it on the fire while Alionushka delightedly threw raw potatoes on the hot embers.

We dined sitting on the thick grass and ate the fat crayfish with a ravenous appetite. We returned home in the clear night, gliding silently over the fields under the moon that lit up the whole steppe with its silvery rays that made the yellowing wheat shine and sparkle.

*Fishing for crayfish in our pond*

FOR THE WINTER of 1909/10 we decided not to go abroad. Instead we left our pleasant Dubrova in September and moved to Kamenka. Of course, after Dubrova the house in Kamenka seemed wretched and we felt very cramped, although we were able to go to the annexes and the buildings attached to the house through our own corridor. But the stables and pigsties were only two steps away and naturally lacking in charm; also, Dubrova had spoiled us for the proximity of other houses and dirty village streets.

We made up our minds to spend Christmas in Dubrova, where we could have a Christmas tree for the children of the staff and for Alionushka. On Christmas Eve the children arrived, and the rest of the staff, about fifteen in all, grey with uncombed hair and wearing miserable old rags. They uttered not a word and showed no sign of joy or pleasure. We had prepared presents for them and Alionushka started to distribute them. They took them without a word, not really knowing quite what it all meant. An embarrassing silence reigned in the room. No one joined in Alionushka's joyous excitement, and they finally left as they had come.

During that winter we had no luck when we went stag-hunting. We never succeeded in getting close enough, even though we saw quite a few fine animals. We were driving back disappointed along the border of the Yurchikha forest, when we suddenly heard the barking of dogs in pursuit of prey. We stopped and our driver Tadeus looked back. "Sir," he said, "those dogs are chasing a stag." But a few moments later the barking stopped. All at once a beautiful hunting dog appeared and stopped when it saw us. There were many stray dogs that fed on wild game and orders had been given to shoot them without pity. Delighted at a reason for loading his gun and furious that strange dogs should be hunting in our woods — not to speak of his dissatisfaction at having failed to shoot a stag — Lev raised his gun and aimed at the motionless animal.

I barely had time to shout, "Lev, don't shoot it! It may be Vassya's dog!" as the shot was fired. The dog didn't budge. Then, having lowered its head as if searching for game, it ran off in the direction of the Yurchikha wood and disappeared. I made the sign of the cross: "Thank God you missed him! If you hadn't, there'd have been a terrible row!"

As we started for home we had moved only a few steps when we came upon a beautiful stag and Lev shot him. Tadeus got down and tied him onto the sleigh at our feet, and we drove home very pleased with ourselves.

But it turned out that the dog had indeed been shot, that it was found dead two days later, and that it was Vassya's best hunting dog. To our astonishment, this led to a court hearing which proved to be so ludicrous that Lev and Vassya made it up and there were no hard feelings.

*Tadeus shooting at the stray dogs that preyed on game and other animals near the Kamenka slaughterhouse.*

60

*The comfortable office we arranged for Lev in the aunts' house*

FOR SOME TIME we had felt that there was something amiss in the way the Kamenka houses were shared out, particularly as regarded the big house and ours, which were run on the same budget. It seemed more logical to have everyone in the same house. Furthermore, there was a lack of housing for the employees. In the large house, despite all Manya's efforts, conditions were primitive. Uncle Nicholas, with his generous nature, did not look into domestic details and simply supported Lev's decisions, even when these were important ones. Once again he entirely approved of the project. "Mariamna knows how to do this. Of course it will be better for you and much easier if you move in with my sisters," he agreed.

Without thinking any more about it, we announced that we were moving into the big house. Our servants, our furniture, our cattle and ourselves, everything was moved there. I also took my own housekeeper, which meant that the old one, Anna Feodorovna, had to be dismissed. The aunts' cook Jacob also went, which helped our diet enormously.

No exterior improvement could be started before springtime, but indoors we started making changes right away. The oak panel that had been in our dining room we moved to Lev's office, and fixed it up attractively with a game of chess on each side and a large writing table. With its claret-coloured walls, the office was very cosy. A lovely red carpet was laid on the floor and curtains hung on the windows.

We loved Lev's office and often stayed there warming ourselves at the fire in the corner.

IN THAT PERIOD before the 1914 War, the way people managed their land was undergoing many changes. I can only speak directly of our own circle, of the city of Kiev and its province, of Kherson and Chernigov, but I believe the same things were happening elsewhere.

Previously the landowners' wives had lived in their estates like reigning princesses, which in some ways they were. They never took any interest in household details; it was even considered improper for them to go into the kitchen or to look into the matter of provisions. Their housekeepers were there for that purpose, and they were given a free hand. My mother had been an exception. She was always deeply involved in the household chores and supervised everything – so that people would laugh, even a little scornfully, when they spoke about her.

My style was rather a different one. I wasn't interested like Mama in all aspects of the household, but I did study very carefully everything that had to do with the farm, and sent my poultry and livestock to shows.

As the general outlook changed, it became a matter of shame to ignore one's household. To behave like a retarded landowner's wife who never paid any attention to her enterprise and was totally devoid of all competence became disgraceful.

Once upon a time, literature and intellectual culture had been the privilege of the aristocratic class, but slowly they were beginning to reach other classes until, at the time I am speaking about, they had become universal. The same thing happened in agriculture. The peasants no longer threw the manure into the ditches but spread it on their fields. They started growing beets in an intensive way. The quality of their cattle improved because we sold them our pedigree calves. Soon interest in their farming enterprise grew.

THE NEXT CHRISTMAS, at Kamenka, winter was well installed and the traditional tree stood once more in the dining room, all decorated with gold trimmings, nuts, tangerines . . . and joy! Aunt Sasha went to church on Christmas Eve with her maid. It was a clear and snow-white evening and the temperature was -3° or -4°C. Christmas carollers ran around the courtyard with a star, peering through the windows and waiting for the moment when they would be let into the house to blare out "The Nativity of our Lord God." At 5 the tree was lit as it was done every year, with only the aunts present and Alionushka putting paper hats on their heads. Aunt Vera sat at the piano and played "Home Sweet Home", and we held each other's hands and danced around the tree singing. Lev returned from the factory emanating heat and the smell of beets.

The New Year! We eat, drink and make wishes! In the morning we are still in bed when the chambermaid Efimy and the housekeeper Anastasia Petrovna, wearing aprons filled with seeds, arrive in our room and throw them on us by the handful while murmuring, "Happy New Year! All best wishes of happiness! May God give a good harvest!" What an adorable custom!

*Aunt Sasha going to church on Christmas Eve with her maid*

1910. Каменка Согольник. M.Davidsff

*Carollers with a Christmas star in the courtyard at Kamenka*

THE WINTER of 1913/14 we spent in Kiev in an apartment we had found there the year before. It was a large, fourteen-room apartment with a little garden that required a great deal of redecorating and repair. I took many pieces of furniture from Matussov, among other things an old red divan that I put in the second hallway. When all the furniture had arrived and all the repairs had been done – this was in November – I went to Kiev for the finishing touches. I ordered the wallpaper and carpets and decided on our living arrangements. The governesses would live in the two rooms on the top floor, and next to them would be Alionushka's bedroom and classroom.

When the others arrived, Lev, Alionushka and all the servants who had not come with me, everything was in place, there were flowers everywhere, the fires were lit and coffee was ready in the dining room. The furniture in this pretty dining room had all been designed by my father for Matussov, and he himself had sculpted the frieze above the fireplace in 1886.

Every time I returned to Kamenka I visited Uncle Nicholas, who no longer felt strong enough to go to the big house in the evening for dinner. At dinner with his daughters and Dr. Zamyatin, who came to see him every day, he felt he was among his own people. I liked to go there. Everything was so decent and respectful, so simple and quiet.

That summer of 1914, we were gradually made aware of the news from Sarajevo. It became real to us when we saw the first class railway carriages full of officers at Kamenka station. Mobilization was at hand. The reservists were leaving and their wives accompanied them to the station. Two days later Lev was also called to Kiev; he was given the duty of preparing the reserve infantry regiment stationed at Akhturk, which displeased him intensely. When I heard about this I went to join him in Kiev.

After accompanying Lev to his train for Akhturk I returned to Kamenka. I went to see Aunt Sasha, then Uncle, to tell them all I had seen. "So now, Mariamna, you are all alone," said Uncle.

"I will take care of the whole concern," I answered, "and I will do it as best I know and as best I can."

In 1914 and 1915 Uncle Nicholas hardly went out of his house any longer, and on 2 April 1916 he died in bed at the age of 89.

*The apartment we rented in Kiev during the winter of 1913–14*

*My bedroom in Kiev*

How many incidents we lived through during the first years of the war in our Kiev apartment, especially in the drawing room. It was a warm and cosy room that lent itself to receptions, but I disliked those parties, and preferred to the provincial snobs the flock of cousins who arrived like little birds for tea at 5.

My bedroom was next to the drawing room. It was a very large room where I had assembled some antique furniture, placed all my trinkets, ordered a made-to-measure bed and hung up my favourite pictures and drawings. One day I drove to Matussov, which we had sold in 1915, and took a lot of the icons that hung on the walls there. I hung all these holy pictures over my bed and in the corner an icon that represented the golden head of Our Saviour, which had belonged to grandfather Vassily Lvovich Davydoff, the Decembrist, who had kept it during his whole exile.

After the important Brussels attack, all seemed calm at the Front. But then disquieting rumours started to circulate. Something seemed to be paralyzing the whole war effort. Yet these events did not affect our personal lives. We were sometimes as many as fifteen at the table for breakfast, and frequently after it I would go into town in our old Mercedes and would only get back home at about 4, when I would find the round table in the drawing room already set for tea and Zossim would bring in the samovar. A sofa stood near the table close to the stove, and I would sit there with my back to the wall, warming myself contentedly as the winter was dark and icy cold.

Early in March, or rather at the end of February, events which we had been expecting for a long time finally materialized. Alionushka had a tutor named Elisaveta Petrovna who had very leftist opinions. One day she was called to the phone and someone said to her, "There is a revolution in Petrograd!"

Several days went by in an atmosphere of excitement and enthusiasm. All my acquaintances were delighted by the turn of events – especially the abdication of the Tsar, that weakling. Maybe now the war would come to an end. But then we learned that the bolsheviks had taken control.

When we went to Kamenka everything seemed unchanged. Aunt Sasha greeted us. Grigory brought coffee and all the servants came to pay their respects. Their faces looked the same, as if there had been no revolution.

I often went there because each day brought something new. My farming enterprise, especially the cattle, was under the watchful eye of a very capable Swede, who made butter and wonderful cheeses. One day I went to the cowshed and took out a pure-bred Swiss cow which I led across the road to the big garden. She was a real beauty, all clean and washed,

*Alionushka and I in the Kiev apartment at the time when the Revolution began.*
*Zossim, from the old days at Matussov, is serving us tea*

*Kamenka: our coachman Sidor wants to know who will be getting this cow*

and I was very proud of her as I led her along and stopped in a little clearing where there was tall grass. She pounced on this delicacy and the juicy grass squeaked under her tongue.

"Here I am," I said to myself, "acting like a simple peasant. I brought her here myself to pasture without being afraid. I even made her cross the road to Kamenno."

Suddenly the voice of the coachman Sidor interrupted my thoughts. He came up to me and, looking at me with piercing eyes, his face all freckled over a red beard, said: "Who will this cow go to when the cattle are shared out?"

This question struck me like a whip. I didn't answer at once but finally, trying to hide my agitation, I said something simple and natural. "They will belong to whoever the provisional government will designate."

A FEW DAYS LATER we went to Verbovka. Yes, Verbovka had also changed. Elisaveta Petrovna reigned there with her hysterical socialist ideas. After tea, Lev's cousin Natasha and I went with her for a walk in the fields. As we gazed at the tender and smiling evening, it was as if all the agitation, the anxiety, the sorrow, existed only in our souls and nature did not share in our emotions. We walked on a well-trodden narrow road that passed through the wheatfields, and the ears of wheat rustled and caressed our faces. I asked Natasha if she thought this land would really go to the peasants. Instead of answering me, she threw a questioning glance at Elisaveta Petrovna, who said, "Of course."

"What are they going to do with this vast amount of land?" I asked.

"The same as you did," she answered with an arrogant look.

"That is quite impossible," I said, feeling that I was starting to boil inside. "They know nothing about the land, and in any case can you just take land from one person and give it to another? Can't they buy it, as they did when serfdom was abolished?"

"Not at all," she almost shouted. "You took it from the peasants so you must give it back to them!"


THE EVENINGS in Verbovka were no longer enjoyable. Our only moment of relaxation was when the Szymanowskis came over from Tymoshovka and Felix played the piano while all the others sat on the terrace, staring at the pitch-black night and thinking sad thoughts.

IN AUGUST 1918 we decided to go to Kiev as soon as possible, but some business affairs delayed us and I didn't want to leave Lev. Excesses were being committed everywhere. For instance, in Tymoshovka, where all the women had left for Elisavetgrad while Felix and Karol remained to try and save anything they could, not a day passed without some muzhik or other arriving, saying he had been sent by the authorities, and forcing them to open the suitcases they had been packing. Poor Felix would be hauled to the rural district office and subjected to all sorts of humiliations.

Aunt Lisa, Aunt Katya and Uncle had all died. Only Aunt Sasha was left, close to her century. She was blind and deaf, and never left her room. She would remain seated, silently knitting "by heart". She knew nothing about the revolution, but felt that something was going on and prayed all the time for her relatives.

The evenings were terrible. We would lock ourselves in, and I personally checked all the windows and doors, and made the rounds of the house. We were scared in the silent house. Those pleasant hours we used to spend in the drawing room were a thing of the past. We were the only ones left.

One night the sugar warehouse was broken into and many sacks of sugar stolen before Lev and a few servants were able to scare away the thieves. The very next day we started packing to go to Kiev. We had to leave Aunt Sasha behind with two women who looked after her, because she was no longer able to leave her bed. Once we left, the houses were invaded by peasants, who began to ransack the estate in earnest. In late November Aunt Sasha finally died. By then the peasants had begun to take the furniture away on their carts and drove triumphantly through the village with all their stolen goods.

We were back again in Kiev in our marvellous apartment. How well I felt there! Everything was peaceful and quiet around us; it almost seemed as if nothing had happened. I invited the Szymanowskis to stay with us, and the evenings I spent with them in the terracotta drawing room were pervaded by a special atmosphere, with the curtains drawn, the lamps lit under yellow shades and huge vases of chrysanthemum on the tables. Felix would play the piano while I set in front of him a glass of marsala, saying, "You may only drink this after you have played the Chopin Ballade."

As refugees appeared, fleeing from the bolsheviks, we took in old friends. I gave up my bedroom and moved into a smaller room on the ground floor. A large window gave on to the garden, and when there was a heavy snowfall the trees were covered by a sort of cotton wool, the sight of which made our thoughts fly to the country.

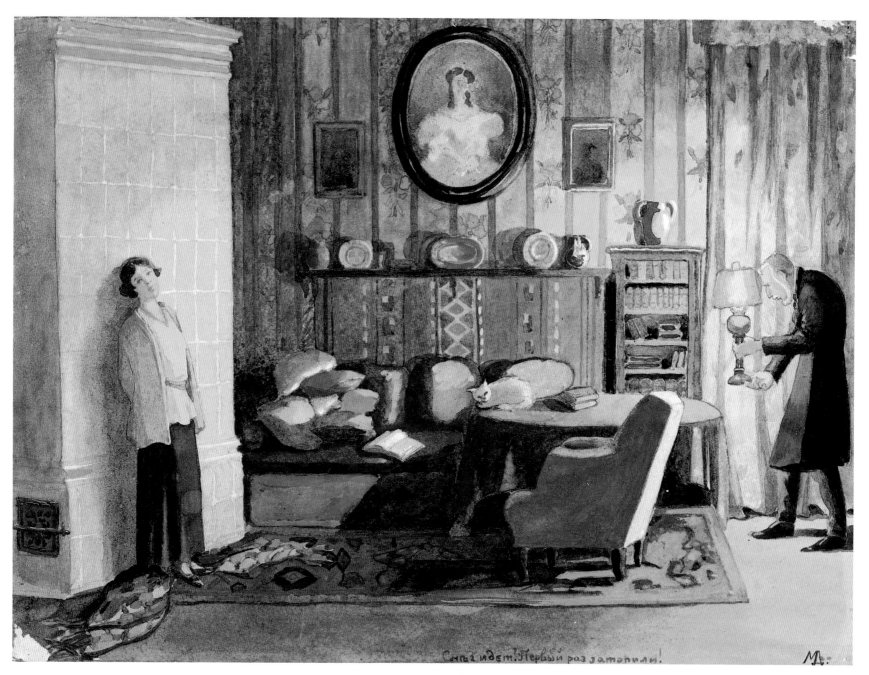

Снѣгъ идетъ! Первый разъ затопили!

*Zossim bringing a lamp as evening falls*

Зимнія птички.

*The long Russian winter: bullfinches and tits at the window, 4 in the afternoon*

CHRISTMAS WE CELEBRATED as always, with a big tree in the dining room. But black clouds were accumulating on the political horizon. People said the bolsheviks were preparing to attack Little Russia, and therefore the Ukraine.

Early in January, there was serious bombardment, making it impossible to go out of doors. Guns could be heard all day long. The Ukrainians were on the defensive. It lasted fifteen days until one night when the noise suddenly stopped. The bolsheviks had entered Kiev.

From then on, fear never left us. People were taken hostage right on the street. Fortunately the reign of terror did not reach us because we lived in a distant section of Kiev, not one favoured by rich people and aristocrats.

We learned that everything had been removed from Kamenka. People were living in the various houses and had taken away the cattle.

After three weeks, the bolsheviks began leaving Kiev, and there were rumours that German troops were on the way. And indeed, in February, Petliura and his men arrived, marching into the city to the cheers of crowds. Order returned immediately, as German patrols appeared every evening. The Germans also invaded the southern provinces and occupied Kamenka, where they forced the locals to return everything they had taken. We got back our possessions and although we never returned to Kamenka, work resumed there.

When the first nice days arrived we decided to rent a villa in Odessa. Food was sent from Kamenka, as in olden times. After a separate peace had been signed with the Germans, our old cook Ivan returned and we also took along two maids, a manservant and a kitchen maid.

We returned to Kiev in the autumn, and in early December we were told that the muzhiks of Kamenka were planning to come to Kiev to see Lev and me and demand explanations about certain private accounts we had with them. Everyone knew the meaning of this kind of interview. Many landowners had been taken away in this fashion, to face outlandish accusations and even death.

After their defeat the Germans left everything and gave up any sort of control. They knew that they would be going away any moment. What action should we take? Lev looked totally downcast but did nothing. We should hide, but where? I decided to go and stay with the Krupinskys, who lived in a fifth-floor apartment on Institute Street in an area called ''Lipki'' that seemed safer than ours. Lev could go to friends of his, constantly changing his hiding place. We waited two or three days more because we couldn't comprehend that such a calamitous thing could happen, but we finally put our plan into action. I would come back secretly at intervals, but even then I was in a hurry to leave. We sent Alionushka to stay with Lev's sister-in-law.

*The "Liebestraum" by Liszt, played by one of the people who took refuge in the Krupinskys' apartment*

"Liebestraum" (List.)

Mysterious agitations started at about that time. At night, from the Krupinskys' apartment we could hear shouting and shots from the street. Who was firing on whom? We hid under our bedcovers when the shooting started, then went to look out the window from which we could see the German camp. One night rockets were fired in the air, and we realized it was the Germans' New Year! The *niania* of the Krupinsky children said, "They will go and it will be a great calamity for us."

In the evening we often sat in the dining room, the windows of which gave onto a courtyard. Ellochka and her husband George, one as charming as the other, did their best to alleviate the sadness of our existence. Fortunately they also had staying with them a man, either a guest or someone in hiding, who was an excellent pianist, and most evenings, as none of us felt like going to bed, we listened to him or to George playing Chopin or Liszt, particularly Liszt's "Liebestraum", which we asked him to play again and again. The sublimity of "Liebestraum" somehow made the reality of our situation disappear in a sad mist.

NOW THE GERMANS were moving out again, and we knew that anarchy would return. When I insisted that we flee to Odessa before the Germans left, Lev agreed, because living in hiding was extremely hard on him. Early in the morning of the day after Christmas, we left by train, feeling nervous and sad and expecting to be arrested any minute.

Our life in Odessa from the end of December to May 1919 was grey and dull. The French were in control of Odessa when we arrived, but we soon heard rumours that they too were planning to leave. That decided us to go to Constantinople. Lev started making the necessary arrangements with the French authorities, which wasn't easy and took a long time. We were finally given our passports and bought tickets on the first ship to leave Odessa, the *Alexander III*. We went aboard that very evening. It was not until the following evening that we departed; it was still light as I stood on deck and watched Russia recede. I felt calmer and a strange weight lifted from me. When there was no longer any sight of land I crossed myself. Goodbye Russia!

*Deeds of years gone by,*
*a legend from the distant past*
(Pushkin)

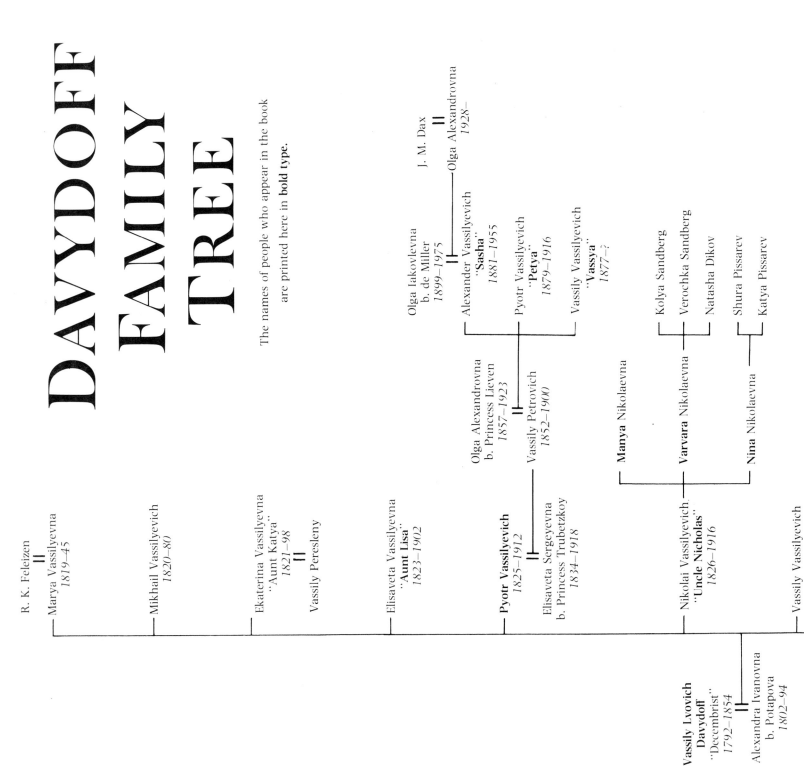

# DAVYDOFF FAMILY TREE

The names of people who appear in the book are printed here in **bold type.**

R. K. Feleizen
==
Marya Vassilyevna
*1819–45*

Mikhail Vassilyevich
*1820–80*

Ekaterina Vassilyevna
"Aunt Katya"
*1821–98*
==
Vassily Peresleny

Elisaveta Vassilyevna
"**Aunt Lisa**"
*1823–1902*

**Pyotr Vassilyevich**
*1825–1912*
==
Elisaveta Sergeyevna
b. Princess Trubetzkoy
*1834–1918*

Olga Alexandrovna
b. Princess Lieven
*1857–1923*
==
Vassily Petrovich
*1852–1900*

Olga Iakovlevna
b. de Miller
*1899–1975*
==
Alexander Vassilyevich
"**Sasha**"
*1881–1955*

Pyotr Vassilyevich
"**Petya**"
*1879–1916*

Vassily Vassilyevich
"**Vassya**"
*1877–?*

J. M. Dax
==
Olga Alexandrovna
*1928–*

Nikolai Vassilyevich
"**Uncle Nicholas**"
*1826–1916*

**Manya** Nikolaevna

**Varvara** Nikolaevna

**Nina** Nikolaevna

Kolya Sandberg
Verochka Sandberg
Natasha Dikov
Shura Pissarev
Katya Pissarev

Vassily Vassilyevich
*1829–73*

**Vassily Lvovich Davydoff**
"Decembrist"
*1792–1854*
==
Alexandra Ivanovna
b. Potapova
*1802–94*

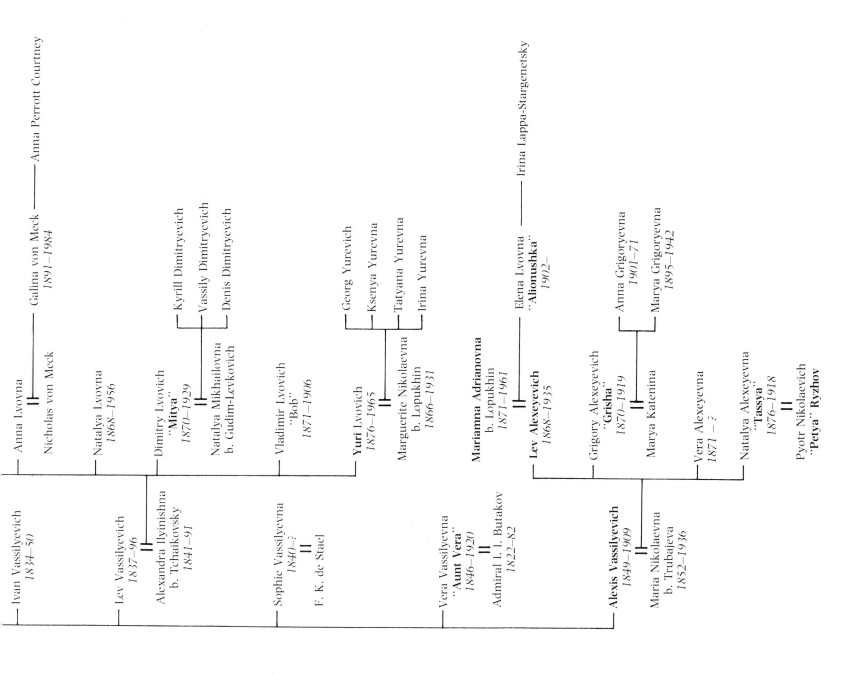

Ivan Vassilyevich
1834–50

Anna Lvovna

Galina von Meck
1891–1984

Anna Perrott Courtney

Nicholas von Meck

Lev Vassilyevich
1837–96

Natalya Lvovna
1868–1956

Alexandra Ilyinishna
b. Tchaikovsky
1841–91

Dimitry Lvovich
"Mitya"
1870–1929

Kyrill Dimitryevich

Vassily Dimitryevich

Denis Dimitryevich

Natalya Mikhailovna
b. Gudim-Levkovich

Sophie Vassilyevna
1840–?

Vladimir Lvovich
"Bob"
1871–1906

F. K. de Stael

Georg Yurevich

Ksenya Yurevna

Tatyana Yurevna

Irina Yurevna

Yuri Lvovich
1876–1965

Marguerite Nikolaevna
b. Lopukhin
1866–1931

Vera Vassilyevna
"Aunt Vera"
1846–1920

Admiral I. I. Butakov
1822–82

Mariamna Adrianovna
b. Lopukhin
1871–1961

Elena Lvovna
"Alionushka"
1902–

Irina Lappa-Stargenetsky

Lev Alexeyevich
1868–1935

Grigory Alexeyevich
"Grisha"
1870–1919

Anna Grigoryevna
1901–71

Marya Grigoryevna
1895–1942

Marya Katenina

Alexis Vassilyevich
1849–1909

Maria Nikolaevna
b. Trubajeva
1852–1936

Vera Alexeyevna
1871 – ?

Natalya Alexeyevna
"Tassya"
1876–1918

Pyotr Nikolaevich
"Petya" Ryzhov